NCAA RECRUIT TIPS:

WHAT 10 YEARS, 70 COACHES, 8 SPORTS, 1 BCS NATIONAL TITLE & 2 HEISMAN TROPHY WINNERS TAUGHT ME ABOUT THE RECRUITING GAME

BY:

@1001RECRUITTIPS

TO MY MOM...
FOR HER UNCONDITIONAL LOVE, ENCOURAGEMENT AND SUPPORT...

LOVE YA!

TABLE OF CONTENTS

CHAPTER #5 - GETTING STARTED

CHAPTER #6 - HELP YOUR CAUSE

CHAPTER #7 - IF 'PLAN A' ISN'T WORKING OUT...

CHAPTER #8 - WHAT TO EXPECT IN HIGH SCHOOL... FROM FRESHMAN TO SENIOR YEAR

CHAPTER #9 - WHAT SEPARATES GOOD PLAYERS FROM GREAT ONES: LEADERSHIP, SACRIFICES AND TIME MANAGEMENT

CHAPTER #10 - FINAL WORD: ALWAYS REMAIN IN CONTROL

GETTING STARTED: THE #1 RULE TO GET NOTICED

"Never mistake activity for achievement."
– JOHN WOODEN

"No one said it would be easy, they just said it would be worth it."

"Impossible is not a fact. It is an opinion."
– MUHAMMAD ALI

"Don't wish it were easier, wish you were better."
– JIM ROHN

SCHOLARSHIP OFFERS: EARNED, NOT GIVEN

THE SCHOLARSHIP OFFER! What is the answer to the million dollar question—what can I do to put myself in the best position possible to get that spot on a roster and a scholarship? Instead of starting this how-to at the very beginning with Step #1, I will start at the end, the moment that you are working so hard to get to! Starting at the moment that your phone rings, you answer it and the coach at your dream school says, "Hey, are you ready??? We'd love for you to be a part of our family, I was calling to offer you a scholarship... what do you say?"

First and foremost, scholarship offers are EARNED—they are not GIVEN. There is no promise or guarantee that a coach will offer you a scholarship, and it's definitely a process that will take you on an emotional roller coaster. You'll laugh, you'll cry... heck, you may even pee your pants as one recruit did during my time helping coordinate official visits! Before you get too deep in the process I just want you to respect the fact that scholarship offers are earned and that you are going to have to prepare yourself to go out there and be in the best position to "earn it!" So here we go...

Nothing is remotely official until a school gives you a written or verbal scholarship offer, preferably a written one! You may be getting a ton of cards, emails and Facebook messages but a coach must give you an OFFER for you to know that they are 100% interested in you. If they haven't offered you a scholarship or tried to get you to campus for a visit (unofficial or official), they're not completely sold on you yet. They may be calling you or sending you mail but they're still just keeping an eye on you... they've heard about you somehow and may be interested!

COACHES ARE LOOKING FOR SKILL, SIZE, SPEED, TOUGHNESS, LEADERSHIP, A RELENTLESS ATTITUDE AND GREAT GRADES.

To many high school players, it seems as if teammates and other players in their town are getting offers every day, that they just fall from the sky for everyone else.

Understand that coaches put a LOT of time and research into making the decision to pull the trigger and offer a player. In most cases, they've scouted you in person at multiple games, discussed it as a staff in depth and have been making calls to their sources in your area to find out more about you as a player and student and more importantly, as a person. They have evaluated your strengths, weaknesses, attitude, coachability, where you fit in to their style of play and if you can get into school academically.

They ask themselves, "Do we have a shot with any other players who are more talented?" (Hey, you wanted me to be honest, right? That's what they're thinking.)

FEARS DISAPPEAR WHEN YOU PREPARE. IT'S FUNNY HOW IT WORKS: WHEN YOU PREPARE AND CHALLENGE YOURSELF ON THE HIGHEST LEVEL YOUR FEARS WILL DISAPPEAR.

The highest compliment a school can give you is to offer you a scholarship, so be very appreciative of the achievement. This means that they see something in you that they believe in. By the end of the process, you just need ONE coaching staff to believe in you, not 50! So when that moment happens, appreciate it!

It's also important to understand that even if you've made a national or state-wide Top 100 recruiting list, that doesn't mean that every college and university will automatically offer you a scholarship. Coaches will be extra diligent in their research, no matter how many ranking lists you are on. The only ranking that they care about is their OWN evaluation of your play, not what some internet blogger thinks!

Most head coaches want someone on their staff to see you play in person before extending the scholarship offer, and they usually prefer to see you play in person for themselves as well. If the head coach isn't able to get there to see you play, they often send a second assistant coach out to cross-check the first coaches' evaluations and what your highlight tape and game film showed. The coaching staff will discuss your abilities and attitude with your prep coaches, coaches who you regularly play against, family and their trusted sources in your area to determine if you are truly the real deal before they extend the offer!

It's important that you never put an expiration date on your dream of getting a scholarship or the chance to play college sports. Too often, players get frustrated early in the process and don't go FIND their opportunities. Life happens for those people who go out and MAKE it happen! Always have faith in yourself, work hard every single day and stay positive while working towards that big chance! I've worked with several coaches who offered players a scholarship just days or hours before Signing Day. Rosters and commitments from other players are fluid – understand it's an unpredictable process, that nothing is final and to be patient! There are plenty of Plan Bs, Plan Cs and Plan Ds that can keep your dream of playing college sports alive!

The recruiting process has the power to turn some players into monsters, some into an insecure, miserable mess. I'm here to tell you to RELAX... STAY POSITIVE... and to HAVE FUN!

If you aren't an internet sensation with 50 offers to pick from, understand that you just need ONE! You just have to find that ONE coach who will believe in you and give you a chance!

#1 RULE TO GET NOTICED

The #1 rule to memorize heading into this process is that in order for a coach to be interested in recruiting you or offering you a scholarship, they MUST see you play—either in person or on tape.

Remind yourself of this over and over every time you find yourself frustrated with the process. We will be going over this in depth shortly and you will be learning multiple ways to make this happen but it is the principle I want you to keep coming back to—COACHES MUST SEE YOU PLAY IN ORDER TO BE 100% INTERESTED!

STUDENT-ATHLETE RESUME

Along with being seen, you will need to put together a Student-Athlete Resume, your profile that will give coaches a quick look at your accomplishments, measurements and contact information. Putting together this profile will be one of your first priorities, a task that you will need to do BEFORE you begin to reach out to coaches.

Below is an example to use as you format your information. When including accomplishments or stats, be sure to put the most impressive notes on top. Coaches and staff can get hundreds of these each week, they may be scanning piles of these, and if your highlights aren't jumping off the page in 20 seconds, they'll likely move on to the next player.

TOP 100 LISTS:

IF YOU ARE NOT RANKED, IT ISN'T THE END OF THE WORLD OR EVEN A SETBACK THAT WILL PREVENT YOU FROM EARNING SEVERAL SCHOLARSHIP OFFERS

SAMPLE #1: STUDENT-ATHLETE RESUME

NAME

#Jersey Number - (YEAR) - Position
Height / Weight / Speed
High School (City, ST)
Phone # / Email Address
HOME ADDRESS: Home Mailing Address, City, St, Zip

ATHLETIC ACCOMPLISHMENTS: (All-State, All-Conference, Team
MVP, School Record, Stat Leader)
ATHLETIC STATS: (Top 4-5 Sport-Specific Stats)
ACADEMIC INFO: GPA / ACT Test Score / SAT Test Score / PSAT
Test Score

HS Coach Name (HS Coach Cell #/HS Coach Email)
High School Name – High School Address, St, Zip

AAU Team Name
AAU Coach Name (AAU Coach Cell #/AAU Coach Email)

SAMPLE #2: STUDENT-ATHLETE RESUME

MICHAEL SMITH
#98- (2014) – Defensive End
6'4 / 240 / 4.85
Thomas Jefferson HS (Honolulu, HI)
222-555-5555 / MichaelSmith98@gmail.com
HOME ADDRESS: 105 Main Street, Honolulu, HI 55225

ATHLETIC ACCOMPLISHMENTS:
Named 1st Team All-County by Hawaii Times
Team Defensive MVP
Lead the conference in sacks (15) and PBU (9)

ATHLETIC STATS:
Junior Season: 15 sacks, 9 PBU, 4 TFL, 2 INT
Sophomore Season: 9 sacks, 2 PBU, 7 TFL, 1 INT

ACADEMIC INFO: 3.5 GPA / 68 ACT score / 1120 SAT Score

HS Coach: Coach Kevin Johnson - 222-555-7777 /
CoachKJohnson@yahoo.com
Thomas Jefferson High School – 1500 South Street, Honolulu, HI
55225

CHAPTER #2

INSIDE THE COACHES' OFFICE

"A good leader takes a little more than his share of blame, a little less than his share of credit."
– ARNOLD GLASGOW

"Continuous improvement is better than delayed perfection."
– MARK TWAIN

"We cannot do great things unless we're willing to do the small things that make up the sum of greatness."
– THEODORE ROOSEVELT

INSIDE THE COACHES' OFFICE: HOW COACHES ASSIGN RECRUITING RESPONSIBILITIES

Nearly every program splits recruiting responsibilities between the staff, primarily by geographic region or by position. Each staff may designate an assistant coach or staff member as the coordinator but normally each assistant coach has an equal responsibility to sign players. One of your first assignments is to find out which coach is responsible for recruiting your area or position at each school that you are interested in.

Many players and parents make the mistake of demanding or waiting to speak to the head coach first, you'll get through MUCH quicker by asking for the coach who scouts your area or position. Unless you are a McDonald's All-American or Gatorade Player of the Year, the head coach probably won't be calling you back!

Once you can get your tape and info to the coach who recruits your area or position (more about this later) and they are impressed and are interested in recruiting you or offering you, they will take your information to the head coach and your recruitment will go from there. Assistant coaches do their research on you before alerting the head coach about you as a potential recruit, that's why it's so critical that you start with them first! In most cases, even if you are able to meet or speak with the head coach, they'll likely forward you or your information to the appropriate assistant coach without spending much personal time on it—this is the chain of command within most teams.

YOUR COACHES WANT NOTHING MORE THAN TO TRUST YOU, NO MATTER WHAT YOU THINK! THEY WANT YOU TO BREAK OUT AND SUCCEED!

Many programs split up the home state, giving each assistant coach an assigned area to monitor and build relationships in. Most schools make it a priority to keep "the best players in the state at home," making sure each of the assistant coaches play a role in identifying ALL potential recruits in the state and building relationships with prep coaches and programs at home. Each assistant is often assigned a handful of counties to become an expert in within the state.

THERE COMES A TIME WHEN YOU MUST PUT YOUR DREAMS AND GOALS INTO ACTION. NO SUCCESS WILL COME OF JUST DREAMS AND GOALS, SUCCESS COMES AFTER YOU TAKE ACTION ON THOSE DREAMS AND GOALS.

In most cases, college coaches still put a lot of attention to in-state high schools even if they currently have no prospects. They are building long-term relationships for the future so that once the school has a great player they will already have close relationships with the coaching staff. They're never just building for that season, they're building for the future.

Major metropolitan areas are usually assigned after that—Atlanta, DC/Baltimore, Dallas, Houston, Chicago, Los Angeles. Key states and regions are assigned from there— Florida, California, Texas, Northeast, Midwest, West Coast and so on. Staffs cover the map—usually including an international contact—so your first priority is identifying these assistant coaches at the schools that you are interested in who are responsible for recruiting your AREA or POSITION.

For example, when an SEC head football coach hires his assistants, they all need strong Florida, Georgia and Alabama ties. They will also need a mix of coaches with ties to the Northeast, East Coast, Midwest, Texas and West Coast. Same thing for West Coast teams, they have assistant coaches with ties across California, Washington and Oregon as well as a mix of staff that has strong ties to the Midwest, Northeast and the South. Each school has a regional focus in recruiting, and each program varies with the level of emphasis that they put on recruiting at a national level, usually dependent on their budget.

Coaches are normally assigned specific geographic regions because it's an area they grew up in, went to college in, have worked in before or have previous ties to. It's also helpful for coaches to have personal ties to those regions: parents of recruits (and their extended families) oftentimes have mutual friends with college coaches which helps in building relationships during the process! It always helps in building relationships if coaches are a friend of a cousin, brother, mother and those ties can go back decades. Coaches want parents and players to feel a built-in familiarity with them, and that has a lot to do with long-term personal relationships. Good or bad, they have a 'track record' in the area.

Most head coaches will say that their priority is to recruit and keep the best in-state players at home, but all major BCS programs will recruit nationally for the best talent possible. Smaller schools may focus more regionally since they have smaller budgets and less media coverage. Smaller schools may focus on prospects within driving distance instead of constantly flying coaches across the country to market their program or regularly flying recruits in on expensive flights.

Long term, established relationships that NCAA coaches have with prep programs are often the reason that many assistants are actually hired. They are able to provide an immediate pipeline to a targeted area, the staff won't have to start from scratch when getting to know high school and AAU coaches in the area. Many coaches have built their careers off the foundation of having a strong history of signing players (and taking care of them while they are coaching them) from certain regions. I've worked with many whose strengths were in their recruiting connections—to Maryland, Washington, DC, Atlanta, Orlando, New York City, Miami and New Jersey.

Once you can identify your recruiting coaches at the schools that you are interested in, get on their radar by sending your highlight tape and Student-Athlete Resume. That is the only true way to get your foot in the door and be taken serious!

INSIDE THE COACHES' OFFICE: HOW THE COACHING STAFF RANKS PLAYERS

Most staffs have a ranking system within their prospect database, a way to rate recruits by their ability or by the level of attention that they want to give them in terms of mail (form letters or hand-written notes), email, calls and what events they get invited to.

Common groups include:
- Players who are being actively recruited (juniors and seniors)
- Top priorities to get a commitment from next (wish list of top recruits)
- Current commitments (recruiting doesn't end even after a player commits)
- Plan B Players (backup plans or players who may be out-of-reach)
- Top Underclassmen who are too young to be contacted
- Players who were evaluated earlier and labeled as 'not talented enough at this time'
- Players who coaches were previously interested in who committed to other schools

Most commonly, each assistant coach has a top list of players that they are 'actively recruiting.' Depending on what time of year it is and where they are in the recruiting cycle, this is the list of prospects that they will regularly call, visit, do research on and try to get to campus for an unofficial or official visit. 'Actively recruiting' is the key phrase, and this group includes players who have already committed to their school, players who have already been offered a scholarship or players who are on the verge of getting an offer.

THERE ARE THOUSANDS OF PLAYERS OUT THERE TRYING TO TAKE THE SAME SCHOLARSHIP THAT YOU ARE DREAMING OF. YOU MUST OUTWORK THOSE PLAYERS EVERY DAY.

Some coaches like to create sub-lists of these top players that they are actively recruiting. This is the group they've already gotten commitments from or players who are on the top of their wish list— the best of the best.

Beyond these two groups, there is often a B-list of players. These are prospects who could potentially be backup offers if the first, second, third or fourth choices don't work out. These prospects usually receive some mail, emails and who may get an invite to junior days, scrimmages or games. This list may also include players who coaches may think are unattainable, players who are long-shots that they may still check in with or mail information to, just hoping for a chance to get their foot in the door.

Beyond those lists, coaches normally keep lists of top unrecruitable underclassmen, players that have committed to other schools and prospects that they determined are currently not talented enough for their program. Coaches keep extra files, even if a player is cut from their watch list, since the statuses of players often changes—players de-commit, get better, have a growth spurt or re-classify grades. I've seen many players cut from our 'actively recruiting' list who re-surfaced months later and were added back on.

In some cases, primarily in football, coaches from other schools may continue to recruit you even if you have committed publicly to another school. Verbal commitments in football aren't always final, so it's common for rival coaches to continue to keep calling, visiting and marketing. If you ever find yourself in this situation and are overwhelmed, you CAN tell these other coaches that you are done with the process and to go ahead and drop you from their list—many will back off after that.

How you are ranked within their database determines how much mail you receive, what kind of mail you receive, which coaches are coming to see you, who's calling you, and what event invites you receive. Everybody isn't treated the same but it's important to understand where you may fit in within the staffs' rankings. Are you a priority to them or are they recruiting several players ahead of you at your position? You need to understand that it's important to keep your options open!

INSIDE THE COACHES' OFFICE: HOW COACHES BUILD THEIR 'WATCH LISTS'

Coaches work off a list of players that they are recruiting, let's call it their 'watch list.' They are constantly adding and subtracting names from their personal list and begin to build one as a staff for each graduating class as early as your freshman year. Separate lists by each group: seniors, juniors, sophomores, freshman and Junior College players. Just because they can't contact you as a freshman or sophomore, that doesn't mean that they aren't already getting organized and doing their research on your class!

Schools may pay thousands of dollars for the databases that they use to help keep everyone organized and connected. Databases are updated daily, players are added and internal rankings are always changing! Many have email features and are able to keep track of more information than you'd ever want to know about.

There are nine main reasons why a coach may begin recruiting you (and add you to the database) that we will be discussing shortly. Once they add you to their watch list and you are a junior or senior (permissible for them to contact by NCAA rules) they may begin to send you mail, request your highlight tape and communicate with you until they decide to make the trip out to come see you play in person and evaluate you for themselves.

HAVING DOUBTS IS NATURAL, WHAT MAKES US HUMAN IS THE ABILITY TO OVERCOME OUR FEARS THROUGH HARD WORK AND HAVING A PLAN.

There is a scramble in the time from when college coaches add you to their watch list... to getting a chance to personally evaluate you for themselves... to getting a feel for your intangibles (attitude, work ethic, academics, family issues), your raw athletic talent and your interest level in their program. Each coaches' watch list of juniors and seniors changes weekly or even daily.

Again, lists for each recruiting class are generated as early as your freshman year. Coaches are constantly adding freshman and sophomores to their database based off observations from games, practices and tournaments as well as from reports produced by regional scouting services that they subscribe to. Coaches are building this list, sending questionnaires to you and researching your contact information so that they will be prepared to contact you once they are legally able to according to NCAA rules.

Don't think that coaches sit around waiting for your junior or senior year to start planning on who they will recruit. Know that college coaches are always three steps ahead in their research and evaluations, and they're always trying to discover the best players in the area before every other college does, and build those relationships with prospects' coaches and high schools first.

These watch lists are the first point of reference that coaches use when planning their travel schedules to evaluate talent during evaluation and contact periods. Coaches take their base watch lists out on the road at the beginning of each evaluation period and will add and subtract recruits based on their in-person evaluations.

For example, each assistant coach may have a list of 25-30 top players on their watch list (who are getting mail and calls) and they are still trying to evaluate another 20 potential players. After those in-person evaluations, they will likely drop five to ten top players but come back with 10 new names to add.

THERE COMES A TIME WHEN THERE'S NOTHING LEFT TO TALK ABOUT. IT'S STRICTLY ABOUT TAKING ACTION. DO WHAT YOU SAY YOU WILL DO.

Again, even if you are on a national or state Top 100 list, that doesn't mean that every coach will think you are a good fit for their system and program. And just because you aren't on any Top 100 lists, it doesn't mean that coaches won't be watching and won't notice you—they are specifically at these events to find the best talent, size and speed. Coaches can sense talent pretty quickly and to them, it doesn't matter if you are a 5-star player or an unranked player. If they like your skills—they will recruit you... simple as that!

Watch lists change daily. You can be dropped with no explanation, at any time, for circumstances you can't always control. On the flip side, know that you can also show up on any coaches' radar overnight, so keep working hard and remain positive!

INSIDE THE COACHES' OFFICE: NO STONE UNTURNED

One of the most common questions or worries that I hear is, "Help, I live in the middle of nowhere, nobody will ever find me" or "My team sucks, nobody will ever come to my school to scout me."

WRONG! This is one of the biggest misconceptions out there!

First off, one of my goals in sharing all of this behind-the-scenes information with you is to get you to stop making excuses and begin to 'find a way' in anything and everything that you do.

Secondly, coaches MUST have a reason to come scout your games or practice—they will rarely just show up unless you play for a powerhouse program that turns out Division I player after Division I player. Of the nine reasons why a coach may begin recruiting you—only one touches on a coach observing you at your high school... so RELAX! There are many other ways to get noticed!

Not all of the players that I've seen sign scholarships over the years were players that our staff found and went after. A good percentage of them were players who came to us first! Players who called us, sent us their highlight tapes, showed up on campus, attended our camps. Many players who are getting recruited got the process going for themselves, they didn't wait for a coach to come find them!

SEPARATE YOURSELF: THE TRUTH IS MOST PLAYERS AREN'T VERY TOUGH. LEARN TO SEPARATE YOURSELF WITH MENTAL AND PHYSICAL TOUGHNESS IN PRACTICE AND GAMES.

Scholarship offers may not just come FIND you... for many of you, you will have to go FIND them!

Many of the coaches that I've worked with are looking for three base traits—skill, size and speed. Many players may only have two of these three traits or they may even only be masters of one. It's up to you to become the greatest that you can be at these three traits and recognize that sometimes you can't control all of these factors... but you can compensate by being really great at the others. After those three key traits, coaches are looking at your intangibles: toughness, leadership, intelligence, a relentless attitude and the ability to make things happen. There are a lot of slow, short players who go on to play at the collegiate level because they find a way to bring value to their high school team by being really great at one or two of these characteristics. You must focus on your skills, size and speed.

COMMITMENT IS A TWO-WAY STREET! YOU WANT YOUR COACHES TO TRUST AND COMMIT TO YOU, YOU MUST TRUST AND COMMIT TO THE THINGS THEY ASK OF YOU.

There are plenty of players that have these key qualities that coaches are looking for that are on losing teams in the middle of nowhere! There are great players who attend schools that haven't EVER produced a player before them who went on to play on the collegiate level. Even if you play in the middle of nowhere and your team can't win a game, that won't necessarily stop you from getting recruited if you have great skill, size, speed, toughness, leadership, intelligence, a relentless attitude and the ability to make things happen.

One of the best examples of this is Anthony Davis, a basketball player from Chicago who went from an unknown player to a top recruit late in his junior year of high school to an NCAA National Player of the Year as a college freshman and eventual #1 overall NBA draft pick. In high school Davis grew from a 6' freshman guard to a 6'8" junior on an unpublicized team that finished with a losing record. It wasn't until the spring of his junior season that he began picking up recognition and skyrocketed to the top of the recruiting rankings. He eventually signed with the University of Kentucky and led the Wildcats to an NCAA National Championship, earning Most Outstanding Player honors.

While many great players can go unrecruited or underrecognized, it is also important to understand that coaches are constantly searching for that next great unknown. They're scouting the area, asking everyone about the next up-and-coming player.

Over and over I've heard coaches say, "I want tremendous players who are winners." This doesn't directly mean they want a player who comes from a school that has produced a lot of Division I players, it means that they are looking for players who come from a CULTURE OF WINNING, players who know how to prepare, players who picked up great habits from successful mentors, who are competitive, who don't make excuses and who won't settle.

Once you get that taste of WINNING... it's addictive. The more of the big games that you have won, the more you will begin to see the game in a different light. You begin to understand what it actually takes to win consistently. You understand the routine, the process. Coaches are looking for players who have already tasted success and want more.

IF YOU ARE TRULY TRYING YOUR HARDEST, NEVER LOSE FAITH IN YOURSELF. JUST BECAUSE THE SHINE AND CROWDS AREN'T THERE (YET), THAT DOESN'T MEAN YOU AREN'T IMPROVING!

Coaches want to know: "Do you understand what it takes to win and are you prepared to make those sacrifices?" What does this mean to you? It means that you can break the mold at your school by being the first player to be able to sign a college scholarship AND it means you can help be the player who helps create that 'winning attitude' at your school. It is up to you and your teammates (not just your coaches) to create a 'Culture of Winning.'

If you are an underclassman, start now and work to be the ONE who initiates the offseason workouts and who encourages their teammates to join them—BE A LEADER. Help create that culture of winning through your work ethic, toughness and by building chemistry within your team.

Prepare to have some thick skin and start going after what you want! Starting right now! Give coaches a reason to come find you.

INSIDE THE COACHES' OFFICE: 14 SIGNS OF A GREAT RECRUITER

Before you get too deep in the recruiting process it's important for you to learn the difference between what it takes to be a great recruiter and what to look for in a coach.

Recruiting players and coaching players are two completely different jobs– and not too many people understand that. Recruiting and coaching require different skill sets. Just become someone is a great recruiter, it doesn't necessarily mean they are a great coach. And there are really great coaches who may not naturally be great at recruiting players.

During the recruiting process, you are only really seeing one side of a coach. Recruiting has become such a critical role in a coach's job description because it has become so competitive nationally, but it's only one-third of their job.

Characteristics of great recruiters include:

#1: A genuine-seeming personality

#2: A master of marketing – 24/7/365

#3: A high-level of organization and attention to detail

#4: A coach who is diligent in their work ethic

#5: The ability to put on a show

#6: The ability to get to know who or what is important in your life and to keep up with what is going on in your world

#7: The ability to create a parent role in your life

#8: The effort of getting to know all of the decision makers and influencers in your life (prep coaches, parents, extended family, mentors, girlfriends/boyfriends)

#9: A confidence about their program, what they can offer you and their ability to get you to commit

#10: The ability to be able to move on to the next player if they aren't getting feedback or interest from their top prospects

#11: Putting together an official visit weekend that will be a home run from your perspective, creating the vision that you have told them that you are looking for in a program

#12: The ability to do skill evaluations without solely relying on rankings or scouting reports

#13: The ability to determine position needs for the team and sign the best available player at that position

#14: Having strong relationships with coaches and programs in their region

Remember—throughout the process you are ultimately looking for a coach who is a great TEACHER. The ability to recruit players helps coaches get and keep their jobs, but the ability to TEACH players is what you are ultimately looking for! Know the difference!

INSIDE THE COACHES' OFFICE:
20 SIGNS OF A SUCCESSFUL COLLEGE COACH

#1: They demand perfection in everything that you do, even off-the-field

#2: They understand that winning is the only thing that they will be judged on and can balance game preparations, strategy and player development with other job requirements that don't necessarily effect wins and losses

#3: They learn from every coach they have worked for and keep everything that has been passed down to them

#4: They are good communicators

#5: They aren't caught off guard on or off-the-field

#6: They demand discipline and are building a team that is disciplined within

#7: They can win versus ranked opponents

#8: Their teams fight back when down

#9: They know how to motivate their players

#10: They have faith and passion in their plan, staff and players

#11: They know how to move on after losses and setbacks

#12: Their players are accountable

#13: They are great teachers and are able to simplify the gameplan

#14: They demand that their players respect the program and the honor of being a college athlete

#15: Their practices are tough

#16: They have strong relationships with other coaches across the sport at every level (high school, college and pros)

#17: They expect their players to graduate

#18: They are prepared for the next step before it happens

#19: They enjoy the process

#20: They know how to manage a staff

CHAPTER #3

A METHOD TO THE MADNESS:
9 REASONS WHY PLAYERS
MAY BEGIN TO BE RECRUITED

"Setting goals is the first step in
turning the invisible into the visible."
– ANTHONY ROBBINS

"Nothing changes if nothing changes."

"When everything seems like an uphill struggle, just think of the view
from the top."

A METHOD TO THE MADNESS

Coaches and programs build their specific 'watch lists' of recruitable junior and senior high school players, and these lists will start to be compiled as early as your freshman year in high school, years before coaches are able to contact or recruit you.

This 'watch list' is their base list, an incomplete list. Circumstances will change from the time coaches may add you to their watch list to when they may begin reaching out to you until you sign that NLI in front of all of your family and friends. These watch lists are fluid and can change daily!

This chapter is devoted to all players—from national Top 100 players to hopeful athletes who may not be getting a lot of attention from coaches by their junior or senior year.

It will never be easy and in most cases, you will have several doors slammed in your face. You WILL have plenty of unanswered phone calls and emails, but I promise these temporary setbacks and hurdles will lead you to the team you are meant to play for. You want to find a team that needs and wants a player just like you! Let's go!

CHAMPIONS DON'T USUALLY WIN ON THE 1ST EFFORT—IT'S ABOUT FIGHTING THROUGH TO YOUR 2ND, 3RD, 4TH, 5TH, 6TH TRY. KEEP TRYING, KEEP FIGHTING FOR WHAT YOU WANT IN LIFE!

9 REASONS WHY PLA' MAY BEGIN TO BE REC

Players may begin to be recruited by college coaches if they...

#1: Were named as a great player by a reputable scouting service on a national or regional report that the coaches subscribe to

#2: Had impressive regional or national combine results (height, weight, speed, vertical, stats, notes) that were sent to the coaches

#3: Were an impressive player at a tournament or game where college coaches were scouting

#4: Were recommended by your high school or AAU coach, especially if your coach has had success throughout their career or has an established relationship with particular college coaches

#5: Stood out as a great player at a college or university camp

#6: Sent a highlight tape to the coaches and they were impressed

#7: Were offered by a rival or comparable school within the conference or region

#8: Are a good friend of a top recruit and could influence that player's school choice

#9: Are the child of a member of an influential group within the university: booster, former player, Board of Trustee member, etc

...ASONS WHY PLAYERS MAY BEGIN TO BE ...CRUITED

#1: Were named as a great player by a reputable scouting service on a national or regional report that the coaches subscribe to

As we will discuss in detail in the next few pages, coaches can find out about you in several different ways. One of the easiest ways that they may get your name and contact information is through national or regional scouting services. These services generate reports from particular regions, events or the ever-popular Top 100 internet rankings.

Being rated in the national or state Top 100 by a fan media site can be a gift and a curse for many athletes. Such rankings may help get your name out there to more coaches but it may also provide you with a false sense of security.

If you happen to be named to such ranks, understand that these lists are only a starting point for most coaches. It may put you on their radar or 'watch list' but it doesn't guarantee scholarship offers or starting jobs. Understand that these Top 100 lists change often and understand that your ranking will definitely rise or fall during this process!

HOW HARD YOU WORK WHEN NOBODY IS WATCHING OR KEEPING SCORE WILL DETERMINE HOW SUCCESSFUL YOU ARE!

On a yearly basis, I've sat in recruiting meetings as our staff would go through Top 100 lists from popular internet sites and disagree with their rankings on many players. Oftentimes, one assistant coach reads off the names and the other assistant coaches respond with "overrated," "ehhhh," "a beast," "overrated," "slow," "good but not tough." You may be impressing fans who waste their days on the blogs but not necessarily impressing the coaches who are extending the scholarship offers. Coaches do their own complete evaluations and your internet ranking plays zero influence on their thoughts of you as a prospective student-athlete!

Coaches use these lists as a starting point. They often drop a few of these 'Top 100' prospects off their watch list after seeing them play in person, or they may prefer one of their teammates or unknown players that they are competing against instead and add them. They may go out and see a highly-recruited internet player and find them too small, slow, out-of-condition, soft or uncoachable and cut them from their list.

Of course, the top three or four players nationally DO usually make an impact earlier in their career but not necessarily everyone else... coaches don't care if you are #26 or #98... or even unranked. They really could care less about your internet ranking!

Other, less public, recruiting services send scouting reports in nearly every sport and geographic region. Most major programs may subscribe to 10 or more of these types of services. Just because a coach with a school-logoed polo isn't sitting in the stands, that doesn't mean that there isn't anyone there watching and taking notes. Coaches get tips about players everywhere, it just depends on if it's a source that particular coach knows or trusts. Coaches depend on these services to help start their research, especially for the key contact information and evaluations they may provide on freshman and sophomore players!

There are likely independent scouts in your region that put together ranking lists for each grade in the area, and sell these lists to several universities. Most scouts include notes (10 words to a paragraph) about your strengths and weaknesses, along with your height, weight, school and contact info. More importantly, they list each player with a recommendation or ranking—DI, DII, DIII, NAIA. Schools use the rankings to separate elite players from good ones, and the good players from the average ones.

At every school and in nearly every sport I've worked in, schools use these reports to find prospects for their level of completion. Reports are generated from everywhere—Mississippi, Kansas, Georgia, Florida, New England, Texas, Illinois, Southern California, Northern

California, Junior Colleges and on International players.

For example, basketball scouting reports will list players as High Major+, High Major, High Major-, Mid-Major+, Mid-Major, Mid-Major-, Low-Major+, Low Major, Low Major-, Division II, Division III or NAIA. Coaches determine what level their school fits on and will look into prospects that fall into their range. They'll add those names to their prospect database, send out a questionnaire, keep an eye out while on the road, maybe request their highlight tape. They may call your coach for more information and to find out their thoughts. Remember, these lists are just recommendations and really just a starting point for coaches until they can get out to see you play in person for themselves.

IF YOU FOCUS MORE TIME ON YOUR FUNDAMENTALS AND LEADERSHIP THAN YOUR INTERNET RANKINGS... SUCCESS WILL COME!

Staffs also cross-reference juniors and seniors on these regional reports to make sure that they haven't missed any late-bloomers or transplanted upperclassmen who have recently moved into the region. Again, the real value in these reports is often in finding the talented freshman and sophomores early or in building a complete list of potential players in the state. Coaches work a year or two ahead in the process and keep an early eye on these top prospects. The earlier they can evaluate these younger players and build relationships with their team and coaches, the better.

If you aren't ranked nationally, it isn't the end of the world or even a setback that will prevent you from earning numerous scholarship offers. If you are a junior and aren't earning offers, it's not the end of the world either—it just means you will have to put in footwork over the summer to get your name out there.

Having been within earshot of daily recruiting calls, I would hear college coaches ask prep coaches often, "Hey, so tell me who's a great player in your area that nobody's talking about." Coaches don't care about the shine, they care about the talent, passion, size and speed... and they want to be the first to discover that hidden gem and they're asking everyone! They leave no stone unturned.

If you are rated #1 in the country or #10 in your school, keep playing hard, training hard and focusing on developing your leadership skills! Ignore your ranking because they play NO influence on whether a school will offer you a scholarship or not! Truly.

College coaches are always looking for great players, but even more desirable is finding great players who are leaders on winning teams. They want players who have a taste of winning and know what it feels like to be successful. It is something repeated over and over during evaluations, "We want great players who are winners." I've heard that from coaches at nearly every school, in every sport. If you focus more time on your fundamentals and improving your team than your internet ranking—success will come. If you are a top team in the state, scouts will come. If you can lead your team to several wins or a state or conference title, it only adds to your chances of being noticed or offered a scholarship.

9 REASONS WHY PLAYERS MAY BEGIN TO BE RECRUITED

#2: Had impressive regional or national combine results (height, weight, speed, vertical, stats, notes) that were sent to the coaches

How do you stack up versus other players in your county, conference and state? Think a smaller version of the NFL combine, if all players were put in a room, separated by position, measured up and put through the same drills, players will begin separating themselves from top to bottom. Attending regional combines will help you get more exposure versus quality players in your area and will especially give you the chance to see how you stack up with measureables. In many sports, size and speed will help get you added to coaches' watch lists without them even knowing about your skill level.

Third-party organizations coordinate combines, showcases and tournaments across the country. From each site, players' heights, weights, speed, vertical jumps, contact info and other measureables are collected. A detailed report from each location (Orlando, Atlanta, Houston, Los Angeles, etc) is sent through a scouting service to coaches at programs across the country, including phone numbers, emails and mailing addresses for each combine participant. Each staff takes the data from each location and will add players to their watch lists accordingly based on their needs. Top measureables (height, weight, speed) are keys to being added to BCS schools, quality regional players are also taken into consideration from each area.

The key benefit about events like the Nike football combines are that they put your name and contact info out there to a variety of coaches. This is EXACTLY what you need if you think you have the skills and want to get noticed. It puts your verified, black and white measureables on a spreadsheet for coaches, along with your direct contact info! That's about as good as it gets, especially if coaches haven't been able to see you yet.

If you truly want to be successful, use these combines or exposure events as a measuring stick during your freshman or sophomore years. This should motivate you to begin to do the extra work that is necessary to be a great college player down the road. These events will be a wake-up call to you that either you need to work harder or they may be a confidence boost that should encourage you to strive for even more, to continue to separate yourself as one of the best. These events will help you get a better idea of where you fit in. Participating in these events at an early age will help you prepare for the common drills that you will be put through during your collegiate career and will help you get over first-time jitters so that when you come back as a junior or senior you know exactly what is expected! You will know

I'M CHALLENGING YOU TO TURN YOUR BIGGEST WEAKNESS INTO A STRENGTH! OVERCOMING THAT INSECURITY IS KEY TO GAINING CONFIDENCE.

exactly what will be asked of you. Don't put too much pressure on yourself at these events but understand there is value in working extremely hard and preparing for these physical tests.

Coaches are always looking for players with the best position-specific skills, but size and speed are base traits that can also help you get on the map. Combines are just one way to get you on the map, but a quick way if you have the right measureables.

9 REASONS WHY PLAYERS MAY BEGIN TO BE RECRUITED

#3: Were an impressive player at a tournament or game where college coaches were scouting

What separates good prep players from great ones is how they perform versus other players in head-to-head competitions. Sounds like common sense—know that you may be the superstar on varsity as a freshman at your school but unchallenged playing with and against weaker competition. How will you compete versus talented players in your area, how will you compete versus older and more physically developed players? Will you out-perform them or will you be dominated? Put all of the players from your state in the ring, players will quickly begin separating themselves. Put those top players from each state in competition versus the best players from the 6-10 states within your region, a handful of players will really separate themselves, and that's the group that elite BCS schools will begin to go after.

THE FEAR OF FAILURE PARALYZES EVEN THE MOST TALENTED ATHLETES. TO DEFEAT IT: PREPARE ON THE HIGHEST LEVEL AND LEAD WITH MENTAL TOUGHNESS.

While many prospects feel their only shot at getting discovered or recruited is if a college coach shows up at their school to watch a game, it's really not that common. First, coaches need a REASON to come to your school to scout you.

Combines will help you get on the map if

you have good speed or size; competitions, events and tournaments will help you get noticed for your skill and technique as well.

In many sports, it is very helpful to play in AAU and compete in regional and national tournaments. These are the events that college coaches put priority on to scout. They bring several players in one location, giving coaches a few days to see a ton of prospects. If possible, try to get on a team and get out there to be seen at these events! That will only improve your chances to get them to come out to your school or to begin to recruit you. Remember, they need a REASON to come see you.

NCAA rules change every year, usually with the intent to limit college coaches to very select evaluation periods. A common complaint coaches have is that these strict rules make it difficult for coaches to get enough good looks at a prospect in action. They may feel that it's not enough time in-person to gather complete information about several players that they are recruiting. Therefore, the system has evolved into third-party events including AAU tournaments and 7-on-7 football tournaments, events that coaches can attend in-person or receive reports or results on.

Coaches know that you may have one or two bad games or practices when they are in attendance. They may hesitate to cut you from their watch list, or they may want to make sure that those one or two beastmode games that you had when they were in attendance weren't a fluke either. So the more they can see (or hear about) you competing with other great players, or the more concrete research that they can get on you from trusted events, the better.

GREAT PLAYERS AREN'T AFRAID OF COMPETITION... PERIOD. ANYONE, ANYWHERE, ANYTIME...

In many sports, combines and tournaments can attract a range of talent and can create these head-to-head competitions that help coaches in the evaluation process. These events are organized to provide opportunities for coaches to sit back, watch and evaluate several players within a weekend. Others events are organized to provide concrete measurements, scouting reports, results and contact information on several prospects to universities across the country, even if coaches are unable to be in attendance to due to NCAA rules. In any way possible, these events provide "exposure" to many prospects and help them get their name out.

It's important to compare yourself to other athletes your age and outwork those players. THIS is your competition. These are the players who want the same scholarships that you want. These are the hundreds of players calling, emailing and showing up on campus with the same dreams that you have.

Be prepared to compete versus better talent and look for the best competition that you can find! Even if you don't match-up, it should motivate you to work harder and understand where you rank. It will pump those competitive juices and eventually you may become just as great as those players who are used to edging you talent-wise.

The drawback during some of these evaluations periods is that coaches have a very limited window of days they can scout these events across the country—too many games in too many locations in a very short period of time. They may already have their list of players that need to be scouted that they are making it a priority to see.

PLAYERS THAT MAKE CONSISTENT PLAYS THROUGHOUT GAMES ARE THE REAL GAME-CHANGERS, NOT JUST THE ONES WHO FOCUS ON MAKING THAT ONE ESPN-TYPE PLAY.

Each sport limits the number of contacts and evaluations coaches may make per prospect throughout the academic year. In sports other than football and basketball, each institution is limited to seven recruiting opportunities (contacts and evaluations combined) per prospective-student athlete. In football, each institution is limited to only six in-person, off-campus recruiting contacts per prospective student-athlete (or their relatives or legal guardians). In men's and women's basketball, institutions are limited to seven recruiting opportunities (contacts and evaluations combined) per prospective-student athlete during the academic year. Each sport has further regulations about when, where and how often coaches may come evaluate you or meet with you, ask your coach or check with the NCAA. Understand that they are limited in the amount of times they may come watch you!

Coaches from every single university are traveling from Atlanta to Kentucky to Las Vegas to Los Angeles to Orlando to Philadelphia to evaluate players during evaluation periods. Coaches from the defending national champions will be at these tournaments... along with staffs from Top 25 schools, from mid-level programs and from teams that may have only won a couple games last year. Every coach is looking for talent, and looking for players that are passionate about playing.

These types of tournaments and evaluation periods are common for all college coaches—all sports. Coaches at the schools that you are interested in may not have the time or flexibility to get to your game if you aren't on their radar already. That's why it's important to try to get on their radar early, to give you more opportunities to be scouted.

IT'S NOT ABOUT YOUR POTENTIAL, IT'S ABOUT YOUR PRODUCTION. HOW DO YOU HELP YOUR TEAM? WHAT DO YOU BRING BESIDES YOUR STATS?

For example, during a men's basketball evaluation period, I know of a coaching staff who went to one city for two tournaments that had 996 combined games scheduled over a three-day period on 47 different courts across town. The first game started at 8am and the last game started at 9:45pm. Almost 1,000 games in three days on 47 courts, you can't imagine the planning and coordination that goes into outlining the most important games to get to and putting together a schedule to make sure that they were getting to see the maximum amount of prospects! Coaches aren't just going to wander aimlessly at these events, they have a specific list of players to scout and a schedule to stick to. They may notice other players while scouting specific recruits but they may not have the time to just wander aimlessly to find players. They have a plan!

Each AAU tournament sells coaches a packet of information with participating player's names and contact info, as well as all the contact info for their AAU coaches. It works simply: when coaches see your talent and are interested, they add you to their list and get in contact with you or your coach. Watch lists undergo a major overhaul during these evaluation periods—cutting several players based on mediocre play, bad attitudes and size issues and adding even more players based on their talent, size, relentlessness and ability to make plays. They aren't just adding scorers, they're looking for defenders, rebounders, ball handlers and players who have a knack for making things happen. They'll come back from these events with thick books of rosters—hopefully with several names circled to add to the database.

Don't focus on your stat line at these events, focus on playing fundamentally solid and hustling on every play. For example, in basketball it's not as much about scoring 40 points in every game as it is about playing fundamentally sound. Don't put too much pressure on yourself to finish with a triple-double, instead you should focus on playing defense, getting rebounds, minimizing turnovers, hustling for loose balls and being a leader. For coaches, it's about finding the most consistent, toughest and fundamentally sound players who play hard and make a difference for their team, especially playing against the greatest competition. They aren't looking for ball hogs. You want to stand out as a difference-maker, what skill can you become a specialist at that will bring value to your team, to a potential college team, that can help you stand out?

When you are the hardest worker, a competitor and a leader at these events... coaches will notice.

9 REASONS WHY PLAYERS MAY BEGIN TO BE RECRUITED

#4: Were recommended by your high school or AAU coach, especially if your coach has had success throughout their career or has an established relationship with particular college coaches

A good place to start during your junior or senior year is with your high school and AAU coaches, they could be a valuable resource to you.

Get their opinion on what level you are most likely going to get looks from—in football are you an elite BCS player, Top 25, BCS-conference caliber, non-BCS, Division II, Division III or NAIA. In basketball, are you a high-major player, mid-major, low-major, Division II, Division III or NAIA material? In ANY sport, ask your coaches where they see you playing at the collegiate level.

If you are a senior, a player who had a serious injury or if you aren't able to qualify academically, are you a player who might do better going to a Junior College first for a year or two?

If your coaches have the same vision that you do and are willing to help, put together a list of the schools that you are interested in and ask them to send your highlight tape and to call the recruiting coaches from those schools to get a read on their interest. Again, get the recruiting coaches name, direct phone number and email address—do the research for your coaches if they are willing to call for you.

Established prep coaches usually have connections with college coaches in the area. If your coach has been at the school for a few years, they've probably built up relationships with college coaches that have recruited that school in the past. If they've been coaching for awhile, they've got connections.

Most college coaches are receptive when high school coaches call about a specific player; especially if you play in a program that has had success or if you are a player from the state. It's good business for college coaches to accept and return phone calls from any and every prep coach and most will if they have the time. Use this gesture of goodwill to your advantage and see if your coach can help you get your foot in the door. There is a decent chance that they can get through to the college coaches and get an honest evaluation on your chances of playing for that school, maybe quicker than if you call yourself. Remember, you need to be realistic and take the recommendation that your coaches give you about the conferences you might fit into.

Remember, this is all just a starting point. Too many players (and their families) get too offended during the process way too early— nothing is ever a final rejection! Thousands of players are underestimated every year and told they belong in less competitive programs than they may actually end up in. You can still keep your dreams alive for playing for Duke Basketball or Alabama Football but you're making a career-threatening decision if you don't at least follow the leads that you may have in the early stages through your high school or AAU coaches.

A prep coach shouldn't make a call to a school that is out-of-reach for you. Prep coaches want college coaches to respect their opinion and won't stick their neck out for you if you really don't have a shot to play for that program. You and your coach want to be taken serious.

TRUTH: SCHOLARSHIP OFFERS ARE NOT GIVEN... THEY ARE EARNED!

From my experiences in major BCS programs, players have come in to my office who wouldn't likely get offers from the local YMCA 30-year-old-and-up league. I would smile, nod my head and send them out the door with my business card. It's important to have dreams but it's also just as important to have a realistic back-up plan. While you are waiting for Coach K, Coach Meyer and Coach Saban to call you back, it never hurts to check out any school in a 300-mile radius.

One of the most critical things to remember is this—don't give control of your recruitment to anyone. Don't get in a situation where you must rely on your current coach for all of your communication and information from college coaches, especially if you are getting interest from several schools. It's nice of your prep coaches to offer to help you but don't let them become your decision-maker, wheeler-and-dealer or personal agent. When you give someone else the control, you open the door to NCAA violations. You will never hear the full story about which schools are interested in you and how strongly these schools are considering you because your 'mentor' may be getting a benefit or reward by steering you to a particular school.

Most prep coaches simply want to help you with the process, while others want to steer you to a particular school for favors or for their personal gain. They don't always have your best interest in mind. If your coaches are trying to put up a wall of communication between you and NCAA coaches and insist that everyone goes through them, unfortunately they don't have your best interest in mind. That's your first red flag! A giant red flag!

Prep coaches are a great contact for college coaches but they aren't always helpful to all programs and opportunities that may be available to you. Recruiting has always been political, and especially in today's climate of bazillion-dollar contracts and marketing deals, some prep coaches want to maximize their power—even if it's not beneficial to you. A small number of coaches are just looking out for themselves, which is exactly why I've written this book TO YOU as a prep player. I want YOU to be able to understand the system to eliminate your dependence on a coach serving as a middle-man (or woman!) for you.

Over the years I've heard several prep coaches talk about "owing a coach a player" or that they "only deal with a few coaches," as if they are making the complete decision for their player. This happens often, and is THE problem.

Being in the circle of an elite athlete puts many people in power positions for the first time in their lives. Some try to act like they are more powerful in the decision than the actual player—RED FLAG!

Every year I would run into numerous players who didn't know our school was interested in them until later in the process because their high school or AAU coaches were unwilling to help provide us with their direct contact info. There are several high school coaches who hide mail from select colleges because they have relationships with coaches at rival universities. It happens all the time and it's not fair to you! It is your right to be aware of EVERY opportunity available to you.

You must ALWAYS stay in control! Each extra layer of "people" coaches must get through is just another opportunity for you to be taken advantage of. YOU will face the suspensions and penalties, not your "people." And most of these characters who claim to be your "people" aren't near as powerful as you think, they may just gain power since coaches know they must go through them to get to you. YOU are the one with the power, no one else.

Lean on your coaches early in the process to help navigate the system. Ask for their advice. But under no circumstance should you ever put them in control of your decision or allow them to be the only point person for you. You could end up in bad situations or be suspended by the NCAA when you aren't responsible for the process yourself. Even if you are shy or scared or have no other family members, never give control of the situation to anyone!

For as many great coaches that I know and have worked with, I would never tell ANYONE where they should go to school and who they should play for. Nobody but YOU should be making that decision based on where you are comfortable.

Keep it simple. The media and marketing companies have made the process a much more pressure-filled situation than it actually needs to be. If you have talent, you can get recruited by your play, not by someone being your agent. You don't need anyone to "sell" you to a university, to "pitch" you to coaches. The only thing college coaches can judge you on is seeing you play in person or on tape. No high school coach or mentor can get a better chance for you in the recruiting process just by their endorsement—but they CAN help get your foot in the door by making a call and sending your highlight tape.

The key to this process is simply a matter of getting an EVALUATION OF YOUR PLAY. If you play well in games, at practice, in camp or on film, you can get the attention of the coaches yourself and give them your direct contact information.

9 REASONS WHY PLAYERS MAY BEGIN TO BE RECRUITED
#5: Stood out as a great player at a college or university camp

By the end of your junior year (or sophomore season if you want to plan ahead), if you haven't been getting interest or offers from many schools, a great way to get on the map is by attending a university camp or two. It's also a great way to network with many other college and high school coaches who may also be able to help you with the process, along with getting the opportunity to see facilities and get a feel for being on a college campus.

Camps are an option to get your foot in the door but you will not directly be offered a scholarship on-site at the camp. NCAA rules prohibit against recruiting during camps, coaches are not able to "extend verbal or written offers of financial aid to any prospective student-athlete during their attendance at a camp or clinic." BUT, it is a good way for coaches to put a name with a face, to give them a chance to see your size, speed and skill in person and for you to get to know the campus, coaches and program better. Offer letters may be sent days or weeks down the road after you have made an impression on the coaches.

10 TIPS TO GO FROM CAMPER TO RECRUIT...

#1 – LET YOUR RECRUITING COACH KNOW THAT YOU ARE COMING AND WOULD LIKE AN EVALUATION: Call the camp office (the phone number should be on the brochure) a couple days before you go and tell the person who answers the telephone your name, position and high school. Ask which coach recruits your area or position. Write down their name and get their direct email address and phone number. Ask to be transferred to them—let them know or leave a voicemail telling them that you are coming to the camp in a couple days (don't call much sooner, they will forget), that you are emailing your highlight tape right now and would like an evaluation, if possible, at the camp. Email them a link to your most recent highlights and include your name, jersey number, high school, position, graduation year, height, weight and contact information along with the camp date that you will be attending. When you arrive to check-in, ask a staff member if your recruiting coach is there and to point them out or see if they are able to introduce you to them. Tell them you are excited to be there say you would hope to get an evaluation and ask if they had a chance to look at the highlights that you sent them.

#2 – NETWORK WITH ALL OF YOUR COACHES: Get to know all of the coaches who are working the camp—not just the coaches from the school that is hosting the camp. Many camps, especially at major Division I programs, have several other college assistants working them, usually from smaller programs. Many coaches from other colleges may be there to network and recruit. They are usually connected to the coaches at the school that is hosting the camp, they may be old teammates, co-workers, friend of a friend or coaches who have previously met at a conference. There are also usually several area high school coaches that are working at the camp, and they may also have leads for you to other college coaches, from all different levels. During meals or down time simply pull them aside and ask them for ADVICE—let them do most of the talking. Tell them, "Coach, I really want to play on the next level, can you give me an evaluation, let me know what you think I need to work on in order to be recruited." This will open the door—some of your coaches may have no leads for you but MOST probably will. Even if you aren't someone THEY are interested in recruiting, most coaches are happy and willing to help and there is a chance that you may be a fit for a school where one of their friends coaches at. Some will be happy to make an introduction or call on your behalf, and you may get recruited from there. NETWORK with ALL of the coaches and simply ask for their advice—see where it takes you!

#3 - TEAM CAMPS: Team Camps are a great way to build chemistry with your team, network with coaches, get a chance to be on a college campus and to see how your team stacks up versus other teams in the area. Team Camps are also usually more affordable than Individual Camps and college coaches may but more emphasis on them as far as recruiting or making evaluations. Talk to your prep coaches or parents about the possibility of getting a group together and fundraising to go to a Team Camp or two, they are definitely great investments for your recruitment and your upcoming season!

#4 - GET A PART-TIME JOB: Camps can be expensive but if you believe you are worthy of being recruited and aren't getting the attention that you would like, they are a TREMENDOUS way to get your foot in the door to find out if there is any interest from a particular school or to network with several college coaches. Unfortunately, due to NCAA rules, no school is able to discount or offer need-based camp scholarships. But, never let money be an excuse—plan early and get a part-time job or find out if your family, church, youth group, athletic league, aunt, uncle, cousin, brother, sister or anyone else that you are close to is able to help you cover the cost of camp. Sessions usually run between $150-$300 for a few days worth of instruction. Think about if there is anyone in your family or life who is able and willing to help you, in most cases there is! It is a really great investment! Camps could be something that you asked for as your birthday present, holiday present or something that you could possibly earn through chores or an allowance. Growing up, NBA great Ben Wallace dreamed of attending a camp of one of his idols, New York Knick Charles Oakley. As one of 11 children in a low-income home, Wallace raised the money by charging neighbors $3 for a haircut, and paid his way to camp.

#5 - CAMP WITH YOUR HOMETOWN TEAM: If you aren't gaining much interest, start with the local universities that are near your home and try to get into their camp. Remember, one of the first questions a coach will ask you is, "Who have you been offered by." Even if it's not your dream school and you are just counting the minutes until you can move far, far away... it always will help you gain interest from other schools if you have a scholarship offer from the hometown team. See #2 - Not only will you be networking with the coaches from that school, you will likely be networking with coaches from other colleges who may have interest in recruiting you.

#6 - PRO-RATE CAMP FEES: Due to NCAA rules, schools are not able to discount camp rates or offer need-based scholarships... BUT, they are able to pro-rate camp fees. If you aren't able to afford the entire amount for a camp that lasts for several days, most schools do pro-rate their fees on a day-by-day or practice-by-practice basis. For example, if a camp is $300 for 5 days, you may be able to attend for one day for $60. You need to make the most of your time at this session—call before you go and let the recruiting coach know that you would like an evaluation if possible (send or bring your film highlights to the camp) and ask for advice from every coach that you are able to be around. Get there early and stay late, eat meals with staff and ask for ADVICE on getting your foot in the door to be recruited. Squeeze as much networking and learning into the day as possible! Learn or ask the coaches for some position-specific drills that you may be able to do on your own to improve.

#7 – COMPETITIVE OR ELITE CAMPS: Many major universities host smaller, more competitive camps that they like to emphasize to the players who they are evaluating or currently recruiting. Due to NCAA rules, camps must be "open to any and all entrants, limited only by number, age, grade level and or gender," so any player who would like to attend (within this limitations) may do so. Even if you haven't been personally invited by the coaches like some of the other players, you are able to attend and can still get your foot in the door with the coaches. A few players get recognized and begin to get recruited this way, so don't worry if you weren't invited or recruited to come like some of the other players. Call each program that you are interested in and ask them if they plan on hosting a Senior Camp, Elite Camp or Competitive Camp for recruits. Sometimes information isn't advertised until a couple weeks before the camp, so continue to check in every month during the summer to find out if they are hosting such an event.

#8 – BEST WAY TO GET COACHES ATTENTION WHILE YOU ARE THERE: Outside of elite skill, size and speed, coaches are always looking for players who are fundamentally solid and who know how to do the dirty work—the acts that help win games that most players don't necessarily want to do or the plays that don't necessary get the media or fan glory. Don't go into the camp trying to make a big ESPN-Top 10 worthy play... go into the camp trying to be the most fundamentally sound and most physical player of the camp. Coaches LOVE players who hustle—players who make the textbook tackle and know how to finish; players who dive for balls, play defense and who can be a difference-maker on the boards; players who aren't just trying to always be flashy but who are always trying to make EACH play that comes their way. Don't focus on making that ONE extraordinary play... focus on making every play count. Coaches aren't looking for flash—they are looking for fundamentals. Want some extra credit? Go out to the field 10-15 minutes early and if the drills are set up (and there are coaches or trainers on the field) get in some extra work, ask for position-specific drills that you can do on your own at home!

#9 – STAY OFF YOUR FEET: If you are really trying to get noticed at the camp, treat it as many college and pro players do—like pre-season training camp. Stay hydrated, eat well and stay off your feet! If you are attending an overnight camp, instead of running around the dorms like a 6-year-old and cannonballing into the pool, get to bed early and give your body some rest so that you will be ready for the next practice. During the season, many college coaches are constantly reminding their players: "STAY OFF YOUR FEET!" Stay hydrated while at practice and make sure to drink plenty of water or sports drinks at all of your meals. Avoid the pizza, junk food and fried foods at the dining hall and stick to the leaner meats, healthy carbs, fruits and vegetables. If possible, bring some extra drinks and bananas to your room to be able to rehydrate during the night. You don't want to lose valuable practice time because of cramps or dehydration!

#10 – TEMPORARY INSURANCE: Most camps will require campers to show proof of insurance—if you aren't covered but still want to participate in the camp, check into temporary policies that usually are very affordable that can give you 30-days of coverage.

Most coaches that I've worked for would at least give you a look at camp if you've gone out of your way to make that initial contact with them and to follow-up at check-in. Coaches naturally enjoy helping players and most will be happy to give you a 5-10 minute evaluation, even if you aren't a player who they will likely recruit.

Bring a copy of your game film or highlights on DVD to leave with the coaches or email links your YouTube highlights with a copy of your Student-Athlete Resume.

They key to making the most of this process is accepting what the coach tells you! Do not get discouraged! Remember—go into camp with an open mind, relaxed heart and good attitude. Remember—when you put pressure on yourself is when you make errors that you wouldn't normally make, so be sure to just RELAX and HAVE FUN! Most coaches truly enjoy helping you!

Make this a positive experience for your recruitment, not a negative one. You should take their evaluations and accept them—they are professionals and have evaluated players on a near daily basis for years. They know EXACTLY what they're looking for in a recruit for their system, style of play and program. You can't argue your way into a scholarship offer—instead, simply listen to their PRICELESS feedback!

Use this time to be productive—get the most for your money! You may only get two minutes of their time (if that) so understand that coaches will be honest and direct with you. Listen to what they have to say. If they recommend that you try smaller programs—do so! If they say they have a buddy who coaches at another school down the road, get their contact info and name and follow-through. It's a foot in the door that you didn't have last week!

Working to raise the money to pay for camp will be just another test of your mental toughness, a toughness that will be challenged daily whether you play Division III or develop into an All-Pro player. All champions have mastered the art of 'finding a way'—and sometimes that starts with finding a way to work your way to camp!

9 REASONS WHY PLAYERS MAY BEGIN TO BE RECRUITED
#6: Sent a highlight tape to the coaches and they were impressed

In most sports, another quick way to get on a school's radar is by sending in a copy of your highlight tape. Remember, the only way a coach can tell if you are worthy of a scholarship offer is by seeing you play or compete—either in person or on tape! If schools haven't come to YOU and if you can't get to their campus for camp, the only other legit way to get their attention, in most sports, is by sending your highlight tape by mail or email.

Some high school coaches can help you put together your highlights or there are services that can also assist you. Either way, it is a step that can greatly help you in the recruiting process.

YOU MUST NOT ONLY BE PATIENT IN WAITING FOR YOUR OPPORTUNITY, YOU MUST BE PATIENT IN YOUR IMPROVEMENTS. GREATNESS OCCURS OVER TIME WITH CONSISTENT EFFORT!

TIPS FOR PUTTING TOGETHER YOUR HIGHLIGHT TAPE

#1: Send highlights from varsity games only

#2: Send recent highlights, games within the last year

#3: Be sure to note your jersey number and jersey color (white/dark) so that coaches can identify you quickly

#4: If possible, send highlights that show you specifically

#5: Include 15-30 plays from multiple games

#6: Keep highlights between 2-5 minutes

#7: If possible, also send 2-3 full or half games. Coaches may request full games in order to evaluate further after you get their attention through highlights.

#8: Show all position-specific skills, you want to show you are a well-rounded player

#9: No music is necessary

#10: No fancy cover is necessary

#11: Be sure to send your Student-Athlete Resume with your highlights (mail or email)

#12: Don't email to generic email accounts, contact the school to get the direct email address of the coach who recruits your area or position

#13: You must follow-up after a week for feedback

#14: If you aren't getting much of a response, contact the team and ask for a grad assistant or Director of Operations or ask to speak with someone who works in recruiting

If you haven't been contacted by the end of your junior year, it's time to put together you highlights early in the summer and begin to send them out to coaches at schools that you are interested in, and several to schools within the state. And for seniors, if you are starting the process late, get those highlights on YouTube and start sending them out—NOW!

Once you have your highlights finished, you can send your tape via email or by mailing a hard copy. Again—your first job is to get the name of the specific coach who recruits your city or position. Get their direct email address and direct phone number. Once you make your list of coaches and get their DIRECT contact info, send it to their attention along with your Student-Athlete Resume and be sure to follow-up within a week or two!

WHEN YOU DON'T BELIEVE THAT YOUR DREAMS CAN ACTUALLY COME TRUE, YOU STOP TRYING! YOU ARE DEFEATED BEFORE YOU HAVE EVEN STARTED!

HOW TO GET THE COACH'S CONTACT INFORMATION AND HOW TO GET AN EVALUATION OF YOUR HIGHLIGHT TAPE

- Find the official athletic department website. Google it!

- Most official university athletic websites have a 'Department Directory' or a 'Staff Directory' link. Find the phone number for the Athletic Department switchboard or the direct number for you specific sport.

- Call the office of your specific team—either directly or call the main athletic department switchboard and ask to be transferred to that specific sport ("Can I please be transferred to the lacrosse office?")

- Introduce yourself and say, "Hi, I am Johnny Recruit and I'm from Nashville, TN and I'm a linebacker at Nashville North Prep. I wanted to send my info to the coach who recruits my area. Could you tell me who that is?"

- Write down the coaches' name.

- Ask for their mailing address, direct phone number and email address. Write everything down.

SCHOOL	ATHLETIC DEPT RECEPTION PHONE NUMBER	RECRUITING COACH (FOR YOUR HOMETOWN OR POSITION)	RECRUITING COACHES' DIRECT PHONE NUMBER	RECRUITING COACHES' MAILING ADDRESS	RECRUITING COACHES' DIRECT EMAIL	NOTES

- Ask to be transferred to that coach.

- If it goes to voicemail: leave your name, grad year, school name and position. Tell them that you are going to email or mail a copy of your highlight tape to them today, say "Coach I was really interested in your program and wanted to know if you could check out my tape and give me some feedback." Tell them you will give them a call in a couple days to follow-up. Keep it short, their voicemail may cut you off.

- If the coach answers, give them the same information, "Coach this is Johnny Recruit and I'm a junior from Nashville, TN and I'm a linebacker at Nashville North Prep. I'm sending you my highlight tape today and was wondering if you'd be able to take a look at it and let me know what you think. I'm really interested in your program." The conversation will go from there—remember, tell them that you will FOLLOW-UP in a couple days.

- Send your highlight tape via mail or email along with your Student-Athlete Resume that includes your name, position, jersey number, height, weight, speed, contact information, high school, travel team information, coaches contact information and grades.

- In two or three days (no longer than that) follow-up with the coach that you sent the information to. "Coach, this is Johnny Recruit from Nashville North Prep, I spoke to you on Wednesday and was wondering if you had the chance to take a look at my tape." If you get their voicemail again, leave the same message. Tell them that you will call back in a few days.

- If after three phone calls you still aren't able to get in contact with the coach, call back the main office and ask if a grad assistant or Director of Operations is available. Start the introduction again from the beginning, get their name, direct email address and phone number. Send your highlight tape to them. Follow-up in a few days.

- If you are a junior or YOUNGER and still aren't able to get feedback, wait a few months. Try back again in the off-season when the coach may have a little more time. If you are a senior, ask one of your prep coaches if they can give them a call to see if they are able to get an evaluation.

Understand that most coaches receive multiple unsolicited emails each day, up to 10 or more a day from players and coaches who reach out on their own! These emails sometimes get lost in the masses of messages in their inbox, especially if they don't recognize your name. Between staff meetings, other more urgent emails from known contacts, practice, issues with current players, workouts, film review and priority recruiting calls, these unsolicited emails can get lost in the shuffle.

Coaches regularly request tapes of high school players on their watch lists, particularly in football. At most BCS schools, if a football coach didn't request the film, they're normally not going to set aside the time to watch it. They simply don't have the time, but don't let this be a dead end for you!

It's CRITICAL that you take the extra step to follow-up with coaches. Many prep players assume their tape was viewed and rejected and never follow-up when truthfully, most unsolicited tapes or emails don't always get watched right away. But if you follow-up on the phone, there is a decent chance that they'll watch it or have someone on staff take a look at it.

Within some programs, a grad assistant or intern is designated to review tapes that are received from players that were not requested, players coaches may know nothing about. If the grad assistant or intern sees something in you, they'll bring it to the recruiting coach to watch it, and if they see something they need, they'll begin to send you mail, call you, come check you out in person or possibly show your tape to the head coach as a potential scholarship player.

These grad assistants or interns are looking to climb their way up in the office ranks and one great way of doing this is by finding future playmakers for their coaches to recruit. Remember, assistant coaches are ALWAYS looking for a diamond in the rough, and if the intern finds that next big one it could mean a promotion for them down the road.

Coaches will NEVER come out to see you play if they haven't seen you on tape first or heard really great things about you from a trusted source. You must give them a reason to come check you out!

WE ARE ALL A WORK IN PROGRESS... YOU JUST HAVE TO BE HONEST WITH YOURSELF ABOUT HOW MUCH WORK YOU ARE PUTTING INTO YOUR PROGRESS!

If your highlights get forwarded on to the recruiting coach and they like you, they'll add you to their watch list and likely make plans to come see you play in person. Simple as that.

Too many players would get transferred to my office who couldn't remember the name of the coach that they'd spoken to a week earlier and it gives off an unprofessional impression. It makes you look like you don't really care and know nothing about the program. When you call, always take notes, you better be sure that the coaches are on the other line!

As an operations assistant, there were times I could barely get two minutes in to ask my questions—so don't be offended that a coach hasn't spent 10 minutes chasing down your tape and watching it. Sorry to keep harping on this but.. they just truly don't have the time. They could strictly watch unsolicited tapes all day and still never finish!

BELIEVE IN ALL OF YOUR HEART THAT YOU CAN ACCOMPLISH ANYTHING YOU DREAM OF... BUT YOU MUST WORK RELENTLESSLY FOR IT EVERY DAY.

Another good thing to remember is that most coaching staffs have a regular routine with their schedule, especially during the season or during organized off-season workouts. In football, every Monday has the same schedule, every Tuesday has the same schedule, etc. Other sports that play multiple games per week have a similar daily routine: morning staff meeting, lunch/exercise break, time to return phone calls, player meetings or film sessions, practice, meetings. Between 11am-2pm is probably the best time to reach coaches in their office, they might not be there the whole time but they should be there at some time during that window, unless it's a gameday!

In most cases, a coach or staff person will take a look at it if they know you're going to call back. They have to prioritize what is urgent in their world first, and that usually involves projects for the head coach, preparing for practice, returning phone calls or an issue with a current player or top recruit.

Once a coach has watched your tape and you are able to get them on the phone or to return an email – the next step is to take their evaluation. In some cases, this may be a quick rejection!

Almost every coach will give you an honest but direct evaluation of your tape. Again, they do this for a living, and probably have been evaluating talent for 10 to 20 years. They know what type of player will fit their system and which will be able to compete and be successful in their conference. They don't always sugarcoat it, so again—don't get defensive, make the most of this opportunity!

I don't know ONE coach who likes telling a prep player that they aren't good enough for their team. IT'S THE HARDEST PART OF THEIR JOB. But... they will be direct with you because it hurts both of you in the long run if they sugarcoat it and lead you on. They don't have the time to spend with you if you keep calling back and YOU need to figure out the next school and coach to contact in order to get on the right path.

But, this is where you can make the most of your opportunity. Ask them ONE more question—"Coach, would you suggest any teams or coaches that are looking for a player like me?"

Some coaches may say no and hang up, but there is a small chance they'll have some leads for you. Again, coaches know other coaches everywhere—so they may have a few schools that you could be a fit for. In some cases, they may even make a call or two or forward your email and highlights for you if they have a relationship with coaches at those other schools—they're usually an old college teammate or former co-worker. They're helping out their buddy and doing their good deed for the day.

If you go into this process and respect the fact that coaches and their support staff are very busy, you can usually get some very good (and free) advice.

The toughest part is actually getting to the right person and being persistent without being annoying! Don't call every day, don't call every week. Don't talk too much, don't tell them your life story. Don't make excuses why nobody has discovered you yet or get defensive or forceful. Don't bother the coach during the season when their schedule is overloaded. DO be patient! DO stay positive!

Keep it short and simple, "Coach, can you take a quick look at my tape and let me know what you think."

IF YOU NEED AN EDGE, SEPARATE YOURSELF DOING THE JOBS NOBODY ELSE WANTS. LEARNING HOW TO SUCCEED AT THE DIRTY WORK WILL GET YOU MOVED UP THE DEPTH CHART.

9 REASONS WHY PLAYERS MAY BEGIN TO BE RECRUITED

#7: Were offered by a rival or comparable school within the conference or region

Another common reason why coaches may look into your abilities is if a rival, conference or comparable school offers you a scholarship. It is very common to hear a head coach go into an assistant coach's office and say, "Hey, the big kid from St. Louis just got offered by School XYZ, what did you think of him?"

Coaches are always keeping an eye on the competition and they also expect their assistant coaches to know about EVERY POSSIBLE prospect in their assigned geographic region or position. They will want to know why that assistant coach didn't think they were worthy of recruitment or an offer... or they will put

SACRIFICE = SUCCESS

that assistant coach into action to get a copy of your film in order to evaluate you for themselves.

If you are offered by a school, you will likely get looks from their rivals or schools within the conference to see if you are someone they should be offering too.

When you begin approaching coaches on your own, one of the first questions they will ask you is, "Who have you been offered by?" Your answer will give them a starting point in their research, so even if it's a less competitive school than you may be interested in, it does give other coaches an idea of your talent.

Never lie about what schools have offered you! Coaches quickly do their research and will find out and possibly eliminate you. There is nothing wrong with saying, "I have no offers yet," it doesn't necessarily mean you aren't talented, it only means you haven't been discovered yet.

9 REASONS WHY PLAYERS MAY BEGIN TO BE RECRUITED

#8: Are a good friend of a top recruit and could influence that player's school choice

This isn't a factor that you should bank on or work to make happen for yourself but I am throwing it in there because there ARE players who earn scholarship offers or opportunities to walk on to a team because of their long-term relationships with top prospects.

When an elite player wants to play with their best friend (who may not be near as talented) there are schools that will make that offer, sacrificing that spot from a more worthy player. They may want to do anything to get an edge in the recruitment or want that elite player to feel their most comfortable with their best friend on the roster with them. Some schools are willing to take the hit, others may not be.

Coaches can see through if the 'best friend' is a true factor in the decision for an elite recruit, never try to shop yourself in this way.

I've only heard of it happening a few times during my career but I AM throwing it out there to offset your frustrations, if you've been around this at your school. It is real. It does happen on occasion. It's something you'll have to get over because it will never change. Instead, let's find a school who is truly excited about YOU!

9 REASONS WHY PLAYERS MAY BEGIN TO BE RECRUITED

#9: Are the child of a member of an influential group within the university

Money talks, power talks and another way that players may find themselves on the roster is if they are the children or relatives of influential people of the program—long-time donors, University Board of Trustees members, former players, professional players, CEOs, celebrities, etc.

Many programs carry one or two players on their roster who are relatives of major boosters, donors or influential people with the university or athletic department, most of them as walk-ons. A coaching staff may begin to send mail and notecards to these prep players but may not be reserving a scholarship, rather simply saving them a spot as a priority walk-on.

Throughout my career I have worked with coaches who have actively recruited and offered players who were very talented, who just happened to be related to influential people or celebrities. Their connections may have nothing to do with why a player is recruited, it could 100% based on their talent.

But, business in any industry still revolves around this type of preferential treatment... that will never change. In the business of big money college athletics, these walk-on positions will always be up for discussion.

If the athletes have legitimate talent and are children of high-profile athletes or CEOs, they may get a few more national scholarships than they normally would, simply for the exposure or buzz it may bring to the program... or for the potential to gain a new financial supporter. A few may be given the chance but many have actually earned it.

Particularly for potential walk-ons, it's important to understand that many of these positions are already spoken for, so becoming a walk-on may not be as easy as you think.

Politics will play their way onto any team and there isn't much you can do about it! Again, it's about finding a school who is excited to have a player like you!

30 FACTORS THAT RECRUITS CONSIDER WHEN SELECTING A SCHOOL

Players choose schools for a variety of reasons, many recruits focusing on a key three or four factors they must-have when making their decision. Below are a list of 30 factors (good and worthless) that players have used when making their decisions:

#1 - Graduation Rates of Athletes

#2 - Class Size

#3 - Academic Support Available for Student-Athletes

#4 - Degree Programs Offered

#5 - The City the University is Located In

#6 - Distance from Home

#7 - Consistent Success of Athletic Department as a Whole

#8 - Athletic Department Budget

#9 - Program on the Rise After Tough Few Years

#10 - Big Name School vs. Small Name School

#11 - Conference and Level of Competition

#12 - Relationship with the Head Coach or Position Coach

#13 - School Spirit

#14 - Style of Play

#15 - Player Improvement / Development

#16 - Team Discipline

#17 - Traditions

#18 - Playing Time – Opportunity to Start

#19 - Facilities

#20 - Draft Record

#21 - Crime Rates

#22 - Visibility to Earn National Individual Awards

#23 - Other Signees

#24 - Attractive Student Body

#25 - Post-Season Opportunities

#26 - Personality of Head Coach

#27 - Opportunity to Win a Championship

#28 - Family Atmosphere

#29 - Two-Sport Athlete Opportunities

#30 – Gear / Uniforms

CHAPTER #4
THE RECRUITING CYCLE

"It is not that the dream is... but what the dream does."

"Be not afraid of growing slowly, be afraid only of standing still."
- CHINESE PROVERB

"It's not that some people have willpower and some don't. It's that some people are ready to change and others are not."
- JAMES GORDON

"If it is important to you, you will find a way. If not, you will find an excuse."

THE RECRUITING CYCLE: FROM BUILDING WATCH LISTS TO FIRST DAY OF CLASS

Like life, like nature, recruiting follows a cycle. There is an information-gathering period, an evaluation period, a getting-to-know-you stage, an offer, a woo-ing stage and a closing stage. At each stage, coaches drop players from their list and begin to narrow down their top targets to a group that they will focus their time and energy on. Here is a quick overview of the cycle:

INFORMATION GATHERING (FRESHMAN/SOPHOMORE):

- Building a Watch List for each graduating class of any potential athlete that would be a fit for the program, as early as freshman year (See 9 Reasons Why Players May Be Recruited)

- Sending questionnaires, updating contact and school info in the database

EVALUATION PERIOD (JUNIOR/SENIOR):

- Calling prep coaches in assigned areas to find out more about the players on current Watch Lists, also adding new unknown players coaches may recommend

- Reviewing highlight tapes and game film

- Traveling to games or tournaments to evaluate players in person

- Inviting players to camps or clinics

- Inviting players to games, Junior Days or unofficial visits

- Evaluating transcripts and grades

- Using social media accounts to learn more about players personalities and mindset on the recruiting process

- Discovering any red flags about prospective student-athletes concerning grades, character or attitudes

- Sending mail and academic information to prospects

GETTING-TO-KNOW STAGE (JUNIOR/SENIOR):

- Getting to know your selection factors, decision timeline and the people who will be helping you make your decision

- Calling you, your family, your mentors and your coaches to stay up-to-date with your life, often non-athletic conversations. The NCAA regulates when and how often college coaches may call you and your family, these rules vary by sport.

- Showing up at your games to show support

- Building relationships with you and everyone that is important with you and who could help you make the decision

- Sending you more personalized academic info, athletic info and personal notes

- Inviting you to campus for an Official or Unofficial Visit- giving you a campus tour, invitation to a campus event or athletic event and making you feel at home

- Answering questions that you may have about their program, university, depth chart and situation. Recruiting is a two-way street and if they are sincerely interested in you, they want you to be just as excited about the decision as they are

- Encouraging you to register with the NCAA Eligibility Center

SCHOLARSHIP OFFER (JUNIOR/SENIOR):

-        As a staff, the head coach will discuss your skills, size, speed, intangibles and academics with the assistant coaches and make a decision to offer you a scholarship. They rank, by position, their preference of players. They play the waiting game of waiting on their top choice to get their commitment, if they aren't getting an immediate yes they will keep their options open. Coaches are often conservative in deciding to offer a player a scholarship.

WOO-ING STAGE:

-        After extending a scholarship offer, coaches will begin putting the press on you, throwing stats and impressive facts at you and will do everything they can do to market their program to you. They want you to feel at home and feel like you are surrounded by family.

CLOSING THE DEAL:

-        Official Visits, paid for by the athletic department

-        In-Home Visits, where coaches make a trip to your house to seal the deal and get a commitment

-        Finalizing the official National Letter of Intent paperwork

-        Finalizing test scores and transcripts in order for you to qualify academically

-        Finalizing all information with the NCAA Clearinghouse

-        Finalizing university admissions, housing and scheduling paperwork

FIRST DAY OF CLASS!

THE RECRUITING CYCLE: CAN YOU QUALIFY ACADEMICALLY

The first question a college coach will ask once they are sold on you as a player is, "Can they get into school academically?"

Before you will be able to accept an athletic scholarship, practice and compete you will need to register with the NCAA Eligibility Center and have your academic and amateur status verified. We will be going into depth about the NCAA Eligibility Center and their standards shortly, but understand that it is critical to plan academically and take your schoolwork seriously.

Admission requirements do vary greatly from school to school, even for athletes. You will have to meet standards within the division (I, II, III) but possibly have to meet an even higher standard at particular schools. Just because you meet the Division I standards that doesn't mean you will meet a particular schools' standards.

Many players may shoot to qualify academically for Division I but they may fall short of the Division II standards and not be eligible for those scholarships. It's best to aim higher academically than to just meet the bottom standards, you may not get a Division I offer and then be stuck because you don't qualify academically for Division II. As of 2013, Division II standards require a minimum SAT score of 820 (only critical reading and math sections combined) or an ACT score of 68 (sum of English, Mathematics, Reading and Science).

ATHLETIC DEPARTMENTS HAVE ACADEMIC ADVISORS WHO PROJECT HOW YOU WILL DO AS A STUDENT AND IF YOU ARE WORTH THE TIME TO RECRUIT. CAN YOU SUCCEED ACADEMICALLY IS DISCUSSED!

Since recruiting is such a time-consuming process for coaches and they are constantly evaluating so many players, if they know you aren't even close to meeting the NCAA's and University's academic standards, they will likely drop you from their watch list and move on to the next player.

To most coaches, you aren't worth their time if they know it will be an issue to get you into school academically. Coaches simply don't have the time to battle for you, it's a process of appeals and special considerations that takes months of attention. Just so you know, in several cases, coaches are also recruiting other players with your same talent who are on track to have the grades to easily qualify.

Academic advisors at many universities may request transcripts of prospective student-athletes from coaches in order to project or predict how recruits will finish high school academically or what deficiencies they will need to take care of while planning for their senior year. They may even have standards in place that can end your recruitment or put your official visit on hold if they don't believe you will academically qualify.

JUST BECAUSE A COACH ISN'T AT YOUR GAME THAT DOESN'T MEAN SOMEONE ISN'T WATCHING! ESPECIALLY UNDERCLASSMAN, PEOPLE ARE WATCHING! LOTS OF OPPORTUNITIES!

Be sure to use the NCAA Eligibility Center code of 9999 when you register for the SAT or ACT to ensure that all of your scores are reported directly to the NCAA Eligibility Center from the testing agencies. Test scores that appear on transcripts will not be accepted!

It is also important to remember that the NCAA GPA (grade point average) is calculated using NCAA core courses only, be sure to look at your high school's 'List of NCAA Courses' on the NCAA Eligibility Center's website. These courses generally fall into the categories of math, science, English, social studies and foreign language. Only courses that appear on your school's list will be used in the calculation of the core GPA!

In my experiences, players aren't held back academically because of a lack of intelligence but rather a lack of effort. Don't let this be you! Your school, the ACT/SAT and college coaches can work with you if you have learning disabilities, concentration problems or credit deficiencies but you must address these issues as soon as possible!

THE RECRUITING CYCLE: MANDATORY STEP REGISTERING WITH THE NCAA ELIGIBILITY CENTER

There is one mandatory step in order to accept a scholarship from a Division I or Division II institution, registering with the NCAA Eligibility Center and completing certification that verifies your academic requirements and status as an amateur athlete.

WHAT YOU NEED TO KNOW ABOUT THE NCAA ELIGIBILITY CENTER...

- You must register with the NCAA Eligibility Center (www.EligibilityCenter.org) in order to practice, play and receive a Division I or Division II athletic scholarship. You may register at any time, but it is recommend that you begin the process during your junior year of high school.

- Academic requirements are not the same between Division I, Division II and Division III. You may qualify for one division and not qualify for another. It's best to be prepared to qualify for all!

- Academic Requirements:
  #1 - Graduate from high school
  #2 - Complete a minimum number of NCAA-approved core courses (varies by division and graduation year)
  #3 - Earn a minimum GPA in those NCAA-approved core courses
  #4 - Earn a required SAT or ACT sum score, dependent on Division I or II standards.

- Only courses that appear on your school's List of NCAA Courses will be used in the calculation of the core GPA. Be sure to look at your high school's List of NCAA Courses at www.eligibilitycenter.org.

- Your SAT/ACT scores must be reported DIRECTLY from the testing agencies, test scores that appear on transcripts will not be used. When registering for the SAT or ACT, use the NCAA Eligibility Center code of 9999 to ensure that your scores are reported directly to the NCAA.

DIVISION I STANDARDS: (Prior to August 1, 2016)

DIVISION I CORE COURSES STANDARDS: 16 Core Courses
- 4 years of English;
- 3 years of math (Algebra 1 or higher);
- 2 years of natural or physical science (including one year of lab
- 1 extra year of English, math, or natural or physical science;
- 2 years of social science; and
- 4 years of extra core courses (from any category above, or foreign language, comparative religion or philosophy);
Note: Courses with similar content may be deemed duplicative by the NCAA Eligibility Center.

- You must earn a minimum GPA in the above required 16 core courses, depending on your graduation year and SAT/ACT scores. (See Sliding Scale on the next page.)

- Time Limitation on Core Courses: You must complete the 16 core-course requirement within four consecutive academic years (i.e., eight semesters) from the start of ninth grade. See the NCAA's website for additional time-limitation guidelines.

- Signees are ruled either as Academic 'Qualifiers' or 'Non-qualifiers':
  - As a Qualifier you are able to practice, compete, receive an athletics scholarship and play four seasons in your sport

  - As a Non-Qualifier you will NOT be able to practice or compete for your college or university during your first year nor receive athletic scholarship aid. You MAY receive need-based financial aid. You may not participate in more than three seasons of competition in your sport. To earn a fourth season, you must complete at least 80 percent of your degree requirements before beginning your fifth year of college.

- The SAT score used for NCAA purposes includes ONLY the critical reading and match sections. (The writing section of SAT is not used.)

- The ACT score used for NCAA purposes is the sum of the following four sections: English, mathematics, reading and science.

DIVISION I STANDARDS: (On or after August 1, 2016)

The initial-eligibility standards for NCAA Division I college-bound student-athletes are changing. Note: College-bound student-athletes first entering a Division I college or university on or after August 1, 2016, will need to meet new academic requirements in order to receive athletics aid (scholarship), practice or compete during their first year.

There will be three possible initial-eligibility outcomes:

• **Qualifier:** May receive athletics aid (scholarship), practice and compete in the first year of enrollment at the Division I college or university.

• **Academic Redshirt:** May receive athletics aid (scholarship) in the first year of enrollment and may practice in the first regular academic term (semester or quarter) but may not compete in the first year of enrollment. The student-athlete must successfully complete nine semester hours or eight quarter hours in the initial term at his/her college or university to continue to practice in the next term.

• **Nonqualifier:** Cannot receive athletics aid (scholarship), practice or compete in the first year of enrollment.

Here are the new requirements for college-bound student-athletes first entering a Division I college or university on or after August 1, 2016:

Qualifier must:

• Complete 16 core courses (same distribution as in the past);
• Ten of the 16 core courses must be completed before the start of the seventh semester (senior year) of high school.
• Seven of the 10 core courses must be English, math or natural or physical science.
• Have a minimum core-course grade-point average of 2.300;
• Grades earned in the 10 courses required before the seventh semester are "locked in" for purposes of grade-point average calculation.
• A repeat of any of the "locked in" courses will not be used to improve the grade-point average if the repeat occurs after the seventh semester begins.
• Meet the sliding scale of grade-point average and ACT/SAT score; and
• Graduate from high school.

Academic Redshirt must:

• Complete the 16 core-course requirement;
• Have a minimum core-course grade-point average of 2.000;
• Meet the sliding scale of grade-point average and ACT/SAT score; and
• Graduate from high school.

Student-athletes who fail to meet the required 10 core courses prior to the start of the seventh semester (seven of which must be in English, math, or natural or physical science), will be allowed to retake core courses in the seventh or eighth semester, which will be used in their academic certification for the purposes of meeting the academic redshirt requirements.

Non-qualifer: Fails to meet the standards for a qualifier or for academic redshirt.

NCAA SLIDING SCALE – PARTIAL LIST

[SEE NCAA.ORG FOR FULL LISTING OF SLIDING SCALE]

DIVISION I PRIOR TO AUGUST 1, 2016...

CORE GPA/ SAT / ACT
3.550 and up / 400 / 37
3.250 / 520 / 46
3.000 / 620 / 52
2.775 / 710 / 58
2.500 / 820 / 68
2.250 / 920 / 77
2.000 / 1010 / 86

DIVISION I BEGINNING AUGUST 1, 2016: FULL QUALIFIER

ELIGIBLE FOR FINANCIAL AID, PRACTICE AND COMPETITION

CORE GPA / SAT / ACT
3.550 / 400 / 37
3.000 / 620 / 52
2.750 / 720 / 59
2.500 / 820 / 68
2.300 / 900 / 75

DIVISION I BEGINNING AUGUST 1, 2016: ACADEMIC REDSHIRT

ELIGIBLE FOR FINANCIAL AID AND PRACTICE ONLY (NOT ELIGIBLE FOR COMPETITION)

CORE GPA / SAT / ACT
2.299 / 910 / 76
2.200 / 940 / 79
2.100 / 980 / 83
2.000 / 1020 / 86

See NCAA.org for the full Division I Sliding Scale, this is only a partial list

DIVISION II STANDARDS:

In order to be a Division II Qualifier (meaning you can accept athletic scholarship aid, practice and compete with no restrictions during your first year in college) you must:

- **A)** Have graduated from high school, **B)** Met the required 2.00 GPA minimum based on the Division II Core Courses (below) and **C)** Scored a minimum SAT score of 820 (only critical reading and math sections) or an ACT sum score of 68 (sum of English, mathematics, reading and science sections).

DIVISION II CORE COURSES STANDARDS: 16 Core Courses [students enrolling Fall of 2013 or later]
- 3 Years of English
- 2 Years of Math (Algebra I or higher)
- 2 Years of Natural/Physical Science (1 year of lab if offered by high school)
- 3 Years Additional English, Math or Natural/Physical Science
- 2 Years of Social Science
- 4 Years of Additional Courses (from an area above, foreign language or comparative religion/philosophy)

Division II Partial Qualifier: If you do not academically meet the standards to qualify, you may be eligible to be a 'Partial Qualifier.' As a Partial Qualifier you can receive athletic scholarship aid and practice at your home facility during your first year but you will **not** be able to compete. To be a Partial Qualifier you must have graduated from high school and either A) have a combined SAT score of 820 or ACT score of 68 **or** B) Achieved a 2.000 core-course GPA in the above 16 required Division II Core Courses. You cannot compete during your first year of college but you can play four seasons in your sport if you maintain your academic eligibility year-to-year.

DIVISION III STANDARDS:

DIVISION III STANDARDS
(ATHLETIC SCHOLARSHIPS NOT AWARDED at DIVISION III):
There is no uniform set of eligibility requirements for Division III schools. Eligibility for admission, financial aid, practice and competition is determined by the college or university.

NAIA STANDARDS:

NAIA STANDARDS (SCHOLARSHIP OPPORTUNITIES):

If you graduate from high school in the spring and enroll in an NAIA institution the next fall, you must meet two of following the three requirements in order to receive an athletic scholarship:

- Achieve a minimum of 18 on the ACT or 860 on the SAT
- Achieve a minimum overall high school GPA of 2.0 on a 4.0 scale
- Graduate in the top half of your high school class

THE RECRUITING CYCLE: THE WOO-ING STAGE

If you are the #1 player a coach wants, they will trip over themselves to make an impression with you and those close to you. They will call, write, fax, Facebook, Skype, tweet, show up and your games... anything to show you that you are their first choice and always in their plans. Some of the best recruiters have a sense of confidence about themselves and are very direct about the fact that they're willing to do anything to chase you down and prove to you that you belong on their campus!

All great recruiters know this—they just need a CHANCE. If you are their top priority and they work relentlessly to recruit you they may get the chance to be in your Top 5. After that, they want the chance to work their way into your Top 3 and maybe even be the school that signs you. Most good recruiters have the first critical goal of just getting you to campus for a visit or a game. To a lot of recruiters, that's their #1 goal. They may feel that if they can get you to their house and can show you what they have to offer, then they've got a shot!

THE RECRUITING CYCLE: CLOSING THE DEAL ON HOME TURF

There are two important events that take place in the recruiting process, both revolving around that 'at home' feeling—official/unofficial visits and in-home visits. To recruiters, there is no place like home!

I will go in to depth in a few pages about the questions you need to get answers to during the recruiting process and during Official and Unofficial Visits, remember that it's very important to get to the campus of the school that you are thinking about committing to before you make your decision. It's best that you go there in person to know what you're getting yourself into—the coaches, the campus, the students, the gameday atmosphere, the city, the dorms... everything! Ideally, you don't want to commit to a university until you've gotten a chance to get to their place and can see how they live!

Compare it to online dating, everyone posts their most flattering pictures, writes great profiles and most times they aren't 100% accurate. Old pictures, exaggerations, their personality is rarely what was portrayed in their 'About Me' section. You wouldn't shop for a spouse on the internet and agree to get married without meeting them! Same for every college program that you are considering— it's very important to see them for your own two eyes before signing anything or committing!

There is always a chance that you may not feel comfortable in the community, with the campus, with the personality of the team or in your situation after meeting with the coaches in person, on campus.

A great sign of interest from a coach is when they're inviting you to campus for an official or unofficial visit. If they're inviting you to their games, Junior Days, other campus events or games—they're interested on some level and what to get to know you better.

Throughout the recruiting process, understand that it's a two-way street. Coaches are consistently evaluating if you are a good fit for their program but THEY also want YOU to do your research, kick in the tires and go for a test drive. They want you to feel a fit with them and know that won't truly happen until you've been to their campus. You need to be evaluating them just as carefully as they are evaluating you!

When coaches are ready to close the deal they will usually make the trip to your hometown for an in-home visit. They want to be on your turf, show you that they can fit in with your family and can tell you what their plan is for you. They have been selling to you but this is a final chance to close the deal with those close to you who may also be influencing your decision.

The highest sign of interest that coaches can show you is by getting you to their house for an official visit and getting the opportunity to come to yours for an in-home visit. They will be trying to close the deal on both turfs!

THE RECRUITING CYCLE: QUESTIONS TO ASK DURING RECRUITING PROCESS

Whether choosing a school as a blue-chip prospect with 50 scholarship offers or as a Division III non-scholarship athlete, it is very important to develop your personal selection criteria that will help you through the process – and prioritize it based on your non-negotiables and your preferences. Before the process becomes overwhelming, what are the core factors that you need to be happy and successful?

There are four core factors that you need to research:
#1: Academics
#2: Town and University Community
#3: Athletic Department
#4: Your Specific Team/Position

It is each COACHES' job to sign the best athletes that will put their program in the best position to win. As a staff, they have clearly defined their 'must-haves' in prospective student-athletes at each position. It is YOUR job to define what you need, to do your research and to ask the right questions in order to put yourself in the best position possible to succeed. Don't forget—your job is just as important as their job during the evaluation process!

Determine the handful of core factors that you will be making your decision off of, and stick to evaluating those! Don't get heavily influenced by the other things that truly aren't important to you! Coaches may be throwing the kitchen sink at you in terms of what they have to offer, but many of those things may not be what is truly important to you in the long run. Don't get distracted!

WHAT SUCCESSFUL PLAYERS KNOW: THERE IS ENOUGH SHINE FOR EVERYONE. QUIT WORRYING ABOUT TEAMMATES STEALING THE SPOTLIGHT, THERE IS PLENTY TO GO AROUND!

Take a page from NFL scouts: they ask receptionists, lunch ladies, trainers, coaches, stadium security guards and anyone else a player may come in contact with to find out their true colors—not just how they act around coaches or perform on the field. An NFL prospects 'true colors' are almost as important as their athletic ability when it comes to breaking down the top talent, how is the player mentally, spiritually and what type of person are they? How do they handle success, how do they handle adversity? How do they act behind closed doors or when the cameras are off and when the recruits aren't around? NFL teams are making decisions between one player and another and investing millions and millions of dollars into draft picks—they need to know about every aspect of their life. YOU should take that same consideration with programs and coaches. It's more about what they're not telling you that you need to look into. Do your research!

Don't let one bad comment or opinion take a school off your list—a lot of dirty recruiting goes on—but listen to PATTERNS. If more and more people have the same reaction to a coach or a program, good or bad, listen. It won't take long to get a good picture when you ask enough people.

Ask several people who personally know the coaches you are evaluating—ask them who they would like their children to play for? Don't let them influence your decision necessarily, but instead you are looking for a PATTERN!!!

10 MUST-ASK QUESTIONS DURING THE RECRUITING PROCESS AND DURING OFFICIAL/UNOFFICIAL VISITS

#1: What are grad rates of your sport nationally, and how do they compare to the schools that you are looking at? Does that university and your specific team graduate their players? What percentage of that teams' players have graduated in the last 5-10 years?

#2: What are the grad rates for the coaches that you are thinking about playing for? Have they made graduating their players a priority over their career? What percentage of that coaches' players (even if they were at another school) have graduated in the last 5-10 years?

#3: Will distance be a factor—do you want to stay within a certain distance from home or do you specifically want to go far away to school?

#4: At some point, ALL players get frustrated with an adversity they face in their athletic career and the first target of that frustration is often living in a city that they don't like. You will need a balance! Do you like what the town has to offer off-campus—outdoor activities, beaches, arts, concerts, shopping, other sports teams, etc?

#5: Are all of the other teams at that school successful within the conference and in post-season play? Is the Athletic Director and leadership happy being competitive or are they able to provide all teams the resources to win? Do all of the teams win on a consistent level?

#6: How many players AT YOUR POSITION do they plan to sign in your graduating class? How many players at your position have already committed, how many slots are left?

#7: What is the average class size? Check the official admissions information from each university for official stats, not just what the coaches are telling you!

#8: If considering several offers, does the athletic department have the resources (booster money/corporate sponsors) to hire great coaches and provide several competitive advantages in terms of resources and operating budget? Is the team "doing more with less" and expecting championships on a shoestring budget or are they providing the competitive resources needed to win consistently?

#9: What is the head coach's personality? Players often mimic their coaches, are they great people? Do they only care about winning or do they truly put their players first in terms of lessons that they are teaching them and standards they are setting? Are they womanizers, cheaters, excuse makers, mentally/physically abusive, etc? When you are spending time with the current players ask them how the head coach treats them once they are enrolled—surprisingly, they will usually tell you the truth, good or bad.

#10: What is their plan for you? No starting job is ever guaranteed, even if they may promise it during the recruiting process. Ask them for their plan and also evaluate the roster for yourself.

MORE QUESTIONS TO ASK DURING RECRUITING PROCESS...

ACADEMICS

- What percentage of classes have fewer than 30 students? Fewer than 50 students? What are the class sizes within your intended major?

- Do they offer a major that you are interested in?

- Can you sit in on a class during your visit, particularly in your desired major?

- What are the freshman year credit requirements? What will be your freshman year required classes?

- What is the coach's or department's class attendance policy?

- Do you plan on taking summer school classes and what is the department's policy on summer school?

- Do athletes have required study hall hours? What is the team's policy on required study hall?

- What is a sample daily schedule like during the season and in the off-season?

- Are tutors available? What technology resources are available to student-athletes?

- Does the athletic department or school help with networking or job fairs?

- Has the team or department had any academic scandals within recent years?

- If applicable, are there special accommodations for students with learning disabilities? If so, what do they include?

- Check out what the other players select as majors—do they put student-athletes in "easy" programs? Are several players majoring in "General Studies" or similar programs or are they in tougher majors?

- If you plan on going to grad school, law school or medical school—are you in a program that will help you accomplish your future goals and get into the programs that you are interested in?

- Is the academic program a national leader? Is that something that is important to you or are you more interested in "hands on" opportunities with internships?

- If you are interested in internships, are you in the right city where you may be able to network and find these positions? Does the school place students in great internships?

- Do major companies recruit students from that university?

THE TOWN/UNIVERSITY COMMUNITY

- Schools are usually either in small towns and have a "college town" feel or are in big cities—are you comfortable? Some big-city people get bored easily in small towns or those from small towns are overwhelmed in big cities—do you like the community you will be living in?

- Are you interested in living in a new place outside of your comfort zone for a few years? Move to big city, move out of big city, major climate change, closer to other family/friends—will you be moving to a city that you've always dreamed of living in?

- There is a good chance that your coach won't be there throughout your entire career (it's the nature of the business)—will you still be happy in that town without the coach you are going to play for?

- If you have a spouse and/or children—how will that play into your decision? Is distance a factor? Will they be moving with you? Can you talk to players at the schools that you are interested that are also married or are parents and see how they are able to manage the transition? Do they offer family housing?

ATHLETIC DEPARTMENT

- What do the other athletes think of the Athletic Director and their interactions with them? Does the Athletic Department have great leadership?

- Is the department improving and always bringing in more resources and improvements? Facilities, technology, new athletic training treatments?

- Are the players respected in the community as positive role models? Do they have a history with legal issues?

- Is the Athletic Department profiting? What is their operating budget and how does it compare to the other schools that you are looking at?

- If the department sponsors several teams, are they stretching the budget really thin or does your team have the resources to succeed and compete within the conference or nationally?

YOUR TEAM

- Is the team on the rise? Is there a strong foundation of quality players already in the system that you can learn from and win with? Are they starting from scratch or are there great pieces already in place?

- Will you have time to develop or will you be thrown into the fire as a freshman and expected to deliver or carry the team?

- What is the record of success of the program in last 5-10 years? If the coaching staff is new, what is their track record of success at previous schools?

- Are there any great leaders or mentors that you can learn from?

- Does the team have the opportunity to be a major upset team, does that excite you? Do they play with exceptional heart and like the underdog role?

- If you are a major football or basketball Division I prospect, does the team charter flights for most of their road games so that you will miss less class time? Do they bring tutors or academic counselors on the road?

- Are there certain traditions that you would like to be a part of at a particular school?

- Are their games televised so that your friends and family can watch you often?

- Is there a path for your team to play for a championship or major post-season opportunity?

- Do you want to be a part of a major regional or national rivalry?

- What does the conference offer in terms of academic prestige, competition, tradition, exposure?

- Is there good attendance at games? Is school spirit important to you?

- Is the stadium close to campus? Is it a place you've dreamed of playing?

- Are the teams disciplined on the field or do they make stupid mistakes? Are they undisciplined off-the field with arrests, suspensions or scandals?

- Are the players accountable to each other and competitive? Do they have a positive attitude, work ethic and desire to get better?

- Can you help recruit a 'super class' of other recruits who can come in and make a difference, especially at an underdog team?

- What are the dining halls like? Do they have nutritionists who will help you with nutrition, vitamins, supplements, etc?

YOUR POSITION

- Are you willing to sacrifice playing time at a smaller school to be able to join a high-major team? Or vice versa?

- How is your relationship with your position coach, coordinator or assistant coaches? They will be your primary teachers in many cases, do you get along and believe in their philosophy? Are they coaches you would love to play for?

- Will you be challenged at that school to become the best player that you can become?

- What is the plan for your development?

- Can you test yourself versus the best competition possible, will you get better?

- How are they as COACHES and teachers? Are their players fundamentally sound? How have their players improved over the years, what results can they show you? Watch film with coaches and see what suggestions they have on how you can improve?

- What strength and conditioning improvements would they like to see you make? What is the ideal weight and speed they would like you at, and what weightroom goals would they like to see you at? How have their players improved in terms of strength, speed and conditioning? Do they get pushed around during games?

- How do you fit in to their system and style of play? Is your position underutilized in their system?

WHAT DOESN'T REALLY MATTER

- Are they the biggest, shiniest facilities? (They won't directly help you win, just maybe help recruiting more players.)

- If you go there, will you have a better chance of getting drafted? (Scouts will go anywhere to find the best players, and the cross the country looking for talent. Playing for particular coaches may help you become more fundamentally sound, develop a championship mentality but more of the impact of your coach, not your logo!)

- Can they help you win a national award like the Heisman, Doak, the Naismith, etc? (No school can help you win!)

THE RECRUITING CYCLE: YOUR DECISION TIMELINE

Be very up front with coaches about your timeline, it's a factor they will work to understand and college coaches will often ask you, your prep coaches, your family and those close to you about. Coaches are trying to understand HOW you are planning to do your research and WHEN you are planning on making a decision.

Think about it... do you want to decide early and get all of the drama over before your senior season or do you want to focus on your season first and then decide after you are done playing? If you are an elite player, most schools will wait as long as you need if they are THAT interested. Some schools may let you know that they have to move on if you haven't decided by a specific deadline. No matter what your timeline is, it's best to be open and honest with the coaches who are recruiting you about your timeline and when you plan to make a decision to commit.

Most coaches will keep it real with you about how long they are willing to wait if you keep it real with them about your timeline and how you want to handle the process. If you don't tell them directly, they'll definitely be asking everyone around you, and those people may not be able to give them the correct answer. They just want to understand you and it's always best if they hear that information directly from you.

On a few occasions, I've worked with coaches who held out for better players and were rejected just days before Signing Day—or at the end of the actual day! That opened the door for one or two other recruits who got the offer after a year or more of waiting. If you are in this situation, you are going to have to be very patient and understand that that offer may never come. It's important that you understand the system and make the best decision possible for you based on your preferences. You may be waiting for that date with a supermodel, and that call may never come. Don't let the great school-next-door get away!

THE RECRUITING CYCLE: PRESSURE-TIME TO COMMIT

Once a coach has scouted you, offered you, had you to campus for an official or unofficial visit there will probably come a time when they will begin to put the pressure on you to commit. The goal of every recruiting cycle is to sign the best player to each available scholarship. This phase is a lot like the weeks before Homecoming... when every guy is trying to convince the prettiest girl in school to go to the dance with them. Every coaching staff wants their #1 choice to say yes and to end any speculation about them having interest in any other school.

Each staff sits down and determines their needs by position for the next few years – where will the team be in one or two years? What spots will be open or what positions do they need depth at? Coaches don't begin this process the summer before your senior year, they begin it during your freshman and sophomore years!

Coaches first look at their roster – our QB will be a senior in two years, are we comfortable with the next guy in line and who will be the backup to him? What positions need better depth? What if someone gets injured? Is there a chance that our freshman center will go to the NBA after next season? Three projected starters on our offensive line will be seniors in two years, who will be in the system by that time and are they ready to lead? Since predicting the future is impossible, all coaches can do is make several projections and base their recruiting needs from there. Normally they put priority on certain positions and little or no priority on others, just depending on who is already on the roster or signed for next two or three seasons.

Once a coach has zeroed in on you and started building those relationships with your inner circle, is getting positive feedback on your interest in the program, there comes a time when they'll start putting some sort of pressure on you to commit. They want to lock you up and focus on the next priority on their list. They'll still continue to communicate with you and recruit you (call you and come to your games) but they'll also want to shift their focus on getting a commitment from the next biggest position need.

As you get deeper in the recruiting process, dominos start falling... similar to the time leading up to the Homecoming. Coaches have a ranked list by position of their needs and wants. Their #1 WR, #2 WR, #3 WR and so on... like the prettiest girls in school. There will come a time when players around the country (or state) start committing and there's a scramble to put the pressure on the best available players. A school may have ranked the top WR target for their system, but if they're getting little positive communication back, and if they know that player is listening to many other pitches, they may go for the 'definite' player who may be a little lower on their list but who will be more likely to commit. Coaches ask, "Who is the BEST player that we can REALISTICALLY get and how long can we wait on our top targets?"

> # WE ALL HAVE THE SAME FEARS AND INSECURITIES— OUR RESULTS DEPEND ON HOW WE RESPOND TO THOSE DOUBTS WE PLACE ON OURSELVES.

There are some cases when coaches will hang on to an extra scholarship until Signing Day or later for a big-time player for their program. Big name programs know that they can hold out until the last minute for that star recruit, and if they are rejected they can still find a great player that will accept the offer down the road.

Everyone wants to go to the dance with the best option—who will say yes—so if coaches aren't getting the vibe that they have a realistic shot with you, they may move on to the next-best player available. You might not have much of a warning, so don't play coy. If you are interested, be up front about it. If you are unsure, tell the coach you are still doing your research. If you are in love with them, let them know before they move on to somebody else!

THE RECRUITING CYCLE: RIGHT TO CHANGE YOUR MIND

Another factor I want to stress to you is that you ALWAYS have the right to change your mind before you sign that National Letter of Intent (NLI). No matter how close to Signing Day, if your heart and gut are raising the red flags on your decision—by all means, follow them! Truthfully, college coaches deal with recruits changing their mind ever year, they will get over it. Most coaches want you to make a decision that is best for you, they understand that if you make a decision that you are not comfortable with in the end, you will likely transfer in a year or two, and that effects everyone involved.

Once you determine your non-negotiable decision factors (academic reputation, conference, location), keep it real with the coaches that are recruiting you. Believe me, if you don't tell them what your decision factors are, someone else around you will and it's best that you speak for yourself!

NEGATIVITY GETS YOU NOW HERE!

Coaches are good with a player who can be up front with them and it's better they know your selection criteria from you directly instead of hearing it from a family member, high school or AAU coach or recruiting website who may misspeak for you.

Most coaches are professionals, they won't be mad at you. Disappointed for their programs, yes, but not mad if you can be up front with them. And most will even tell you to reach out to them down the road if you change your mind, they understand this may be a confusing and overwhelming experience for you and will pick up where they left off if you decide to re-open your recruitment down the road.

It's crucial you determine your decision factors and follow your heart! If you don't, coaches know you will be unhappy and eventually transfer from the program. They were all your age once! Keep it real with them and they will keep it real with you!

At the end of the day this is YOUR decision and you need to do what is in YOUR heart, do what makes YOU happy!

IT DOESN'T ALWAYS HAVE TO BE YOU AGAINST THE WORLD— STOP PUSHING THOSE CLOSE TO YOU AWAY. THERE ARE PEOPLE IN YOUR LIFE WHO WANT TO HELP.

CHAPTER #5

GETTING STARTED

"Tell me my dreams are unrealistic, I'll tell you yours aren't big enough."

"You will never win if you never begin."
– ROBERT SCHULLER

"Empty pockets never held anyone back. Only empty heads and empty hearts can do that."
– NORMAN VINCENT PEALE

"Don't let yesterday use up too much of today."
– CHEROKEE PROVERB

GETTING STARTED: DON'T PAY SERVICES TO GET YOUR NAME OUT TO RECRUITERS

Here is a tip to save you a few bucks—Never pay a recruiting service to send your information to universities, especially larger Division I schools.

First off, this book will teach you to find the contact information that you need and to put together your own Student-Athlete Resume and highlight tape.

Secondly, particularly at competitive Division I programs, stacks of athlete resumes aren't taken serious or even looked at in most cases. If you have to pay someone to send out your profile, you must not be that talented. True or not, that is the impression it gives off.

Put together your Student-Athlete Resume, your highlight tape and mail and email them off to the schools that interest you. You can find all the contact information that you need within a few clicks online. And, coaches like players who can show SOME initiative and do some of this work on their own.

Personally, I would discredit these resumes that were paid for and sent in bulk, and very few coaches actually looked at them or added their information to their watch list or to the database. From my experience at BCS Division I schools, I don't remember a coach handing me one to add that prospects' info to the database, ever! But they often handed me ones that players, parents or prep coaches had put together themselves to add to their own watch list.

Sure, they were used more at some of the small programs that I worked with but players would have gotten the same responses if they would have mailed in their own letter and resume. Send it on your own and they will be more likely to read it! Those companies have no extra leverage that you don't have yourself!

GETTING STARTED: THE FIRST QUESTION COACHES WILL ASK YOU

You finally get a college coach on the phone or in front of you! You are halfway there! After the introductions and small talk, one of the first questions that they will ask you is, "What other schools have offered you?"

PAUSE. Don't worry, there are no wrong answers to this. Some of you may say, "Texas, North Carolina, Virginia Tech, Syracuse, Florida State and a few others I can't remember." Others may say "Elon and James Madison," "Temple, Rice, Sacramento State," or "Western Carolina, North Carolina A&T, Florida Atlantic." And even more recruits may say, "Nobody yet." Remember—there is no wrong answer to this question. It's like the chicken or the egg debate, SOMEONE has to be the first to offer you! Hey, maybe one day it will be this coach you are talking to!

This quickly gives coaches a good idea of your ability, it's a reference point for them. If other schools have already done their research on you and found SOMETHING in you, your 'dream' school may be more willing to take a look too. But, even if you have no offers—that doesn't mean they'll immediately reject you—they will probably just ask you to submit a highlight tape or invite you to camp.

COMPETITORS: STAY READY FOR YOUR GOLDEN OPPORTUNITY, IT WILL COME!

Never lie about what scholarship offers you have because coaches can find out within minutes, and it will only eliminate you from their list if they catch you in a lie. Coaches DO double-check your offers, usually the minute they hang up the phone!

The next thing college coaches will want to know (especially if you have no offers) is which schools have tried to get you to campus for an unofficial visit or camp, or which programs have come to see you (not one of your teammates) play or practice. Remember—just because you haven't been OFFERED, that doesn't mean other schools may not be INTERESTED. Coaches may still be doing their research on you, so other coaches who you are reaching out to may ask you which schools are scouting you, inviting you to unofficial visits, Junior Days or camps.

Be up front but never make excuses! The worst thing you can do at this point is lie or give coaches a long list of why-nots... "the coach hates me," "my mom hates me," "my team sucks." Even if your coach hates you, your mom is trying to interfere with the process and your team didn't win a game last year—never start making excuses! Ever!

If you haven't had much contact or feedback from college coaches, get some exposure at regional or national combines or tournaments. Give coaches a list of past and future events that you have or will attend, and they will be able to get an idea of your talent level from those invites as well.

Don't bother with the, "see what happened was..." and just tell the coaches the truth—"I'm just now starting to reach out to schools, here is my highlight tape, stats and contact info, can you take a look and let me know what you think?" Period, skip the rest!

GETTING STARTED: START LOCAL

Since one of the first questions a coach will ask you is "Who have you been offered by?" you'll be taken much more seriously if you can give them some names! If coaches know that you already have offers, it tells them that you have some level of talent and other coaches have already done some research on you.

It's much more efficient to start with smaller programs and potentially work your way up to more competitive programs than by starting the process trying to chase around the defending national champions for an offer. Start small first, then if you are getting positive feedback—go bigger (if that's your dream).

All coaches keep an eye on good local and state players—so if a certain recruit is getting a lot of mid-major attention, there's a good chance that some of the bigger schools may come do their research too.

Too often, I would get calls about players who had no offers at all—that's just a waste of everyone's time. It will be much easier for you to get your foot in the door with UNC, NC State, Wake Forest and Duke if you are a prep player from North Carolina and getting offers from UNC-Wilmington, Western Carolina, Catawba and North Carolina A&T.

LEARN WHAT IT MEANS TO BE RELENTLESS: 'I WILL NOT BE DENIED.'

Coaches want to recruit the best talent they can find—players that other schools usually have interest in too.

Once you begin to get feedback from coaches about what level you can compete at, check out multiple schools at that level. Build momentum, continue to play hard and potentially work your way to other, more competitive schools that interest you if you dream of playing major college sports.

Personally, I attended a small school that was Division II (I-AA football) when I enrolled, and I had the best four years of my life there. Don't eliminate smaller schools who are interested in you, you may be missing out on a once-in-a-lifetime experience!

GETTING STARTED: TIMING IS EVERYTHING

Entering your senior year of high school, take a look at the rosters of the schools that you are interested in. What will the roster look like when you are a freshman? Are they loaded at your position or are they starting jobs going to be wide open?

Take into consideration players who are redshirting, players who will most likely leave school early for the draft and players who will be graduating... Where might you fit in on the depth chart? This is exactly how coaches base their needs, what position will we be thin at? They ask themselves, "What is our biggest need?" They'll also ask: "What position has the most depth? Are we even recruiting for that position?"

When you begin to get a chance to talk to coaches at different schools, ask them how many players in your graduating high school class—at your position—do they plan to sign? How many players at your position have already committed? In some cases, they may not plan on signing any players at your position, so you could be wasting your time, especially if it is late in your senior year.

Coaches get daily inquiries from talented recruits—but who play position that they are no longer recruiting for that signing class. If a school has four scholarship QBs who will still be on the roster by the time you get there, then it's not likely they will sign another. If a basketball team is guard-heavy, they will be looking to add bigs in the next class. Do the math! Ask the coaches, especially if you are a senior!

Life is about timing—and if your position isn't needed at the time, it'll be a big waste of your effort if you're chasing a school that has no need for your position. Keep an eye on transfers, players kicked off the team or de-commitments of recruits at your position but also be smart enough to look at other schools that have a NEED for you.

TRUST IS EARNED THROUGH EVERY DAY HARD WORK, IT IS REALLY THAT SIMPLE.

CHAPTER #6
HELP YOUR CAUSE

"Discipline is doing something you don't want to do but nonetheless
doing it like you love it."
– MIKE TYSON

"A wise man will make more opportunities than he finds."
– FRANCIS BACON

"It's hard to have a good day with a bad attitude or a bad day with a
good attitude."
– JOE MOORE

"Watch the little things; a small leak will sink a great ship."
– BENJAMIN FRANKLIN

HELP YOUR CAUSE: WHAT MAKES YOU UNIQUE

If you are looking for an edge in recruiting, a way to separate yourself from the other players at your level and to climb into the next level of competition—think about how you can become unique, how can you separate yourself? What can you become a specialist in?

Sure, all coaches are looking for scorers and elite speed and size. But as every player chases the leading scorer title, starting pitcher title, leading rusher title, think about other ways that you can separate yourself, especially by doing the work that few players want to do—the dirty work. The rebounding, the blocking, special teams... the list goes on and on.

NEVER FEEL POWERLESS. YOU ALWAYS HAVE THE POWER TO WORK HARDER AND PREPARE HARDER, DROP THE NEGATIVE ATTITUDE!

Not only do I know college players who earned scholarships this way but I know college players who went on to have long-term professional careers because of this approach! What can make you unique? What can you become a specialist at? Free throws, steals, blocking, punt returns yards after the catch, ball security, breaking the first, second, third tackles consistently. Are you the go-to guy on third-down conversions—not necessarily the deep ball guy but the guy who consistently move the chains on third or fourth down?

Do the dirty work that most other players don't want to do and you will have a better opportunity to be discovered and promoted up the depth chart. Take pride in your specialty!

In basketball, in nearly every interview you can hear coaches complaining about rebounding. Very few coaches are ever content with how they do on the boards, even if they are winning the battle in most games. And, undoubtedly, those basketball teams that are in championship contention... they are head and shoulders better in rebounding than every other team. Coaches are searching to find a player who can get them a major rebounding and defensive edge while most players are just concerned with their points per game average. THERE is your chance to become a difference-maker, a starter or even a scholarship player!

Every sport provides similar opportunities... think about the skills that you can bring to a team that aren't what every other player is chasing but will help your team win games. THAT will be a way to create buzz and may help you get recruited.

HELP YOUR CAUSE: DIRECT LINE OF COMMUNICATION

Contact the schools that are interested in recruiting you or that you have an interest in and give them your contact info and ask to have a questionnaire sent to you. If you are in contact with any coaches, give them your home address, home phone number, cell phone number and email address so they can send you information and call you directly.

Some high school coaches hide mail from their players and don't always pass along phone messages that coaches leave. If you are a great player, there may be other schools out there that are interested in recruiting you that you may never hear about. If certain coaches have tried to make contact with you or anyone in your circle, call the school and give them your direct info!

Each year I reached out to several coaches to get direct contact information for their players and would get about 25% of them telling me that we need to go through them directly to speak with the player. There's always another group of coaches who don't respond at all. With technology, our coaches could

IF YOU DON'T WANT TO BE TRIPLE-CHECKED ON, JUST DO THE THINGS THAT YOU ARE EXPECTED TO DO THE VERY 1ST TIME YOU ARE ASKED. NOTHING MORE, NOTHING LESS.

reach out to them on Facebook and get their contact info directly. Players whose coaches kept us from them were happy to hear from us when we went around their high school coaches! In many cases, when the coach finally gets in touch with the player, they had no idea we were interested. Not every prep coach is looking out for your best interested and sharing all of the information with you.

Nobody should be blocking this knowledge from you so it's best if the college coaches know how to contact you directly to avoid this issue.

HELP YOUR CAUSE: RESPOND TO QUESTIONNAIRES

At every program I've worked we've gotten daily calls, letters and emails requesting a questionnaire. This isn't usually a helpful or efficient way to get on a coach's radar, particularly at many Division I schools. Again, the only true way to get the school to recruit you is if they see you play in person or on tape.

The exception is if a school SENDS you a questionnaire, a questionnaire that you didn't call and request yourself. You should definitely fill it out and return it, it means they have gotten your name from a trusted source and want to do some more research on you and may contact you at some point.

On the flip side, when you call and request a questionnaire, it may not get looked at or added to the database when you return it. When people request questionnaires they are often coded before they go out and are not always evaluated when they are returned, particularly at more competitive schools.

Cut to the chase and send your film!

HELP YOUR CAUSE: DON'T BECOME A PEST

Calling or emailing a program every day is a quick way to get noticed, but not in a good way. Your biggest allies in the process can be the staff that answer the phone and generic emails, so it would be in your best interest to not become a pest. They quickly recognize you and soon stop passing your daily messages along.

Programs get daily calls from players and their families telling them that they are the one and only school that they want to play for. While it's a nice gesture, that means nothing to those coaches if they aren't interested in your talent. For this reason, one of the most important factors that I will stress to you is that a coach can't evaluate your talent and offer you a scholarship (or a walk-on spot) without seeing you play in person or on tape first. What does that mean to you? It means that blowing up the phone lines will not help you. Get your highlight tape ready BEFORE calling or emailing coaches at schools that you are interested in and save yourself some trouble.

One of the best pieces of advice I heard about preparing for a job interview was that you need to convince the hiring manager that THEY need YOU—not that they need to hire you because

SUCCESSFUL PEOPLE KNOW THIS: YOU CAN'T COMPLAIN YOUR WAY OUT OF YOUR PROBLEMS—YOU HAVE TO WORK YOUR WAY OUT!

you really need or want the job, employers could care less about YOUR needs and wants during the interview process. Employers want the best and most talented person for the job. Same with coaches. Coaches need to NEED a player with your skills to be interested in recruiting you. Just because it's your dream to play for a certain school, it doesn't mean that they will have any added interest in recruiting you if you don't have the talent to compete there and be successful for their program.

So, once you get your tape ready to mail or email your #1 goal will be trying to get SOMEONE there to confirm that it's been received and to get SOMEONE to watch it. You need to follow-up with them a day or two after it arrives and confirm the name of who will be watching it. If you aren't getting any feedback, you need to call back and see if you can get in contact with a grad assistant or Director of Operations and see if they are able to watch it. This should take you no more than three phone calls!

DRAMA ATTRACTS DRAMA... SUCCESS ATTRACTS SUCCESS

Too often, players will call multiple times per day... FOR DAYS. This is a big DON'T—you will become "that kid." Same goes for parents and coaches—it's unnecessary to call 5 times in a week. It won't help your cause!

If you aren't getting any answers from the recruiting coach or grad assistant, back off and call back in a few weeks. If you are not a senior, back off and call early in the off-season once the coaches may have more time.

As discussed earlier, it never hurts to have one of your prep coaches call. It's good manners for college coaches to call back prep coaches, so use this gesture to your advantage. If you didn't have any luck getting someone to evaluate your tape, ask your current coaches if they will call on your behalf. Remember—a coach probably won't (and shouldn't) call schools for you that are way outside of your talent level. Be realistic when asking for favors— but if your coach agrees to call for you, it would never hurt your chances!

HELP YOUR CAUSE: HOW TO CARRY YOURSELF WHEN APPROACHING COACHES

As you prepare to contact schools, realize that you need to present yourself in a polished way when speaking to college coaches. College coaches are professionals; they may wear sneakers and t-shirts at practice but most of them wear ties or polos at work, and slacks and dress shoes in the office.

I get weekly phone calls from players saying, "Aye, aye.... Write this name down. Yo, John Smith. Write that name down."

Just so you know, I don't even pick up a pen. If you're THAT good, we already have your name in the system and are trying to get in contact with YOU. Or my favorite, "Who's the head coach? Yeah, yeah... Coach Jefferson, let me talk to Steve..."

That extra attitude, ego and unprofessionalism will get you nowhere!

First off, you called us and you shouldn't EVER refer to a coach by their first name. Ever. If you're really interested in a school, look up the head coach's name before you call. Your first goal is to have the person that answers the phone take you serious, and that starts with being polite and organized.

WHEN YOU CONTACT SCHOOLS, MAKE SURE THAT YOU:

• Speak up , speak clearly and don't mumble

• Know the head coach's name before you call or even better, have a list of all of the coaches in front of you so you can make sure you get the name right. Never ask for them by their first name.

• Ask which assistant coach recruits your area and get their name, direct office number and email address. Double-check the spelling and keep notes!

• Spell your name out if leaving a message and repeat your phone number twice. If we can't understand the phone number, nobody can call back!

• If necessary, set up a different email address for recruiting purposes. I can't tell you how many inappropriate email addresses (and Twitter names) I've come across over the years, and ladies, you are just as bad! Keep it simple with your name and jersey number. Also, no mascot names in your email address. If you are Gamecock17@recruit.com, do you think the Clemson and North Carolina coaches will take you serious? Keep it simple: jen15@hotmail.com, bobbysmith@gmail.com or shortstopsam@yahoo.com.

• Depending on your grade, understand that a coach may not be able to respond to you. Rules vary for each sport as far as when coaches are able to contact you so check NCAA.org for that information.

• When you are using form letters, triple check that you have changed everything. I can't tell you how many letters I have received from prospects who in the first line confessed that they were "dreaming of" playing for our biggest rival. We all know coaches AND recruits send form letters, just make sure to check that each separate packet is correct before you mail them!

• If you are meeting a coach, dress appropriately. Nothing will make a coach take notice quicker than if you are wearing a tie and collared shirt or polo. Same for the ladies—cover up and dress for church instead of dressing for the club! Sure, it's okay if you wear something more casual, but coaches will take ANY player serious if they present themselves in a professional way.

CHAPTER #7

IF 'PLAN A' ISN'T WORKING OUT...

"My success wasn't so much due to my intelligence, but the fact that I stuck with problems longer."
– ALBERT EINSTEIN

"When you get to the end of your rope, tie a knot and hang on."
– FRANKLIN D. ROOSEVELT

"Failure defeats losers, failure inspires winners."
– ROBERT KIYOSAKI

"You cannot change your destination overnight, but you can change your direction overnight."
– JIM ROHN

IF 'PLAN A' ISN'T WORKING OUT: NEVER PUT AN EXPIRATION DATE ON YOUR DREAMS

To some the recruiting process will be more than frustrating and to some, the rejection and feedback (or lack of response) may be too much.

Remember—you just need to find that ONE coaching staff who believes in you, not earn 50 scholarship offers from schools across the country. You may not even start (or finish) as a scholarship player—but the goal of playing college athletics on any level is something you should never give up on!

I'm here to tell you : NEVER PUT AN EXPIRATION DATE ON YOUR DREAMS! You may have to start out at a Junior College, or as a walk-on with no scholarship. You may have to try out to be a walk-on two or three times. You may never see game action until your senior year... you may never hear the announcer call your name during starting lineups... BUT, what you will have is a lifetime of memories and most likely, a lifetime of lessons.

FRUSTRATION IS NATURAL. THE QUESTION IS: HOW LONG WILL YOU LET THAT BITTERNESS EAT YOU UP? USE ITS POWER TO MOTIVATE!

Along with the wins, the scholarship money and maybe even the TV time... college athletics are more about the relationships with your teammates, coaches and university, about the memories and about the lessons you've learned that will help you in your adult life.

You must WORK for what you want, stay positive in your persistence and always keep the dream alive, no matter what anyone says!

IF 'PLAN A' ISN'T WORKING OUT: IF THERE IS A CHANGE IN COACHES

One of the toughest hurdles a player will go through during their career is dealing with a coaching change, especially at the collegiate level.

Whether a coach retires, leaves for another school, decides to go coach a pro team or gets fired—emotions run high and the media and critics will pile on the negativity.

DIVISION I, II, III... YOU CAN FIND GREAT COACHES, TEAMMATES AND EXPERIENCES ON EVERY LEVEL! GO WHERE YOU ARE WANTED, HAPPY AND HAVE OPPORTUNITIES!

With traditional and social media being so instantaneous, one of the toughest aspects of a coaching change is the fact that players nowadays rarely hear about the change directly from the coach themselves. When players hear it from ESPN, Twitter or friends texting them, they're naturally caught off guard and usually feel disrespected or shocked. Off the bat, they have a tendency to act out emotionally: lash out in the media, skip team meetings and workouts, stop going to class or threaten to go pro. This is normal and natural, people are trying to make decisions based on EMOTIONS.

It's important to understand that the high rate of turnover in the coaching profession is the prime reason why it's so important for players to feel comfortable at the SCHOOL and in the TOWN without the coach that recruited them there because there is a good chance that the coach may not be there for their entire career.

It's hard for 18-21 year-olds to fully understand but when a coach decides to leave a program, the decision has nothing to do with the players. Coaches take and leave jobs for the pure reasons of #1- the betterment of their family (more money, closer to family and home, a promotion) or #2- a better opportunity to win (bigger budget, bigger fanbase, easier path to a championship). Those are the only two reasons; it is never personal with the players.

It's natural and okay for you to be hurt and frustrated, understand that it is okay for you to take time away from the media, social media and speaking publicly on the matter until you have had enough time for it to sink in and for the university to hire a new coach, you will have time to evaluate the new hire and decide if you would like to keep firm on the commitment or re-open your recruitment.

Early in my career, a coaching change would have been shocking. One of the biggest things that could happen! After my 15 years in athletics, I now understand that it's just part of the business and nearly every team will lose at least one coach every year. It's just the way of life for coaches. Having worked for so many, it'd be safe to say that over 75% are looking for other jobs or being contacted for new positions each off-season, it's just the way it is.

While fans and administration put a lot of their focus (and rightfully so) on the players, there's a whole backbone of the program going through turmoil when there is a transition in head coaches—the assistant coaches, strength coaches, trainers, video coordinators and team operations staff. A head coach is basically responsible for the livelihood of 6-15 full-time staff members and each of their spouses and children. No matter the reason they are gone, nearly everyone else is left hanging and worrying about their job and family. In most cases, everyone lands on their feet but it's a rough few weeks or months until everyone is able to secure a new job.

"LIFE IS NEVER GONNA GET EASIER, BUT EVERY DAY I MUST FIND A WAY TO GET STRONGER!"

The outgoing coach may bring some staff with them and it's understood that the incoming coach has 100% freedom to clean house from top to bottom and bring in their own network of trusted staff. Everyone is on their own during this time, these stretches can bring out the worst side of people and have a tendency to be really, really awkward.

Give yourself time to decide if you are still excited about your opportunities and the direction of the program, it's perfectly normal for you to keep quiet on the matter and have 'no comment' to media and friends, especially if you are a major Division I prospect. Evaluate the opportunities, community and entire situation before making comments you may regret in a week or two!

Understand that in the end you will all be fine, just give the situation time to run its course!

IF 'PLAN A' ISN'T WORKING OUT: JUNIOR COLLEGE

If you aren't getting the scholarship offers that you want or feel you should be getting by the end of your senior season, one of the final options to think about is to attend a Junior College for a year or two. Junior Colleges feed major BCS programs and hundreds of other schools every year with talented players who are able to step into starting positions. You are basically able to re-do the recruiting process once you are enrolled and competing at the Junior College level.

DID YOU KNOW... SUPER BOWL MVP AARON RODGERS HAD ZERO DIVISION I SCHOLARSHIP OFFERS COMING OUT OF HIGH SCHOOL

Aaron Rodgers, Deion Branch, Al Harris, Jeremy Shockey, Chris Johnson, Bryant McKinnie, Duane Starks, Javon Walker and Cam Newton are just a few football players who went to Junior College at some point during their college career and went on to find tremendous success in college and the NFL. Many other NCAA teams recruit from Junior College programs as well.

Along with going the JuCo route for a year or two to basically re-do the recruiting process, some prep players must go that route in order to get the required grades and test scores needed before they can enroll in four-year institutions. Junior Colleges are definitely an option to consider if you feel you are a late-bloomer, had an injury or if you fell short academically.

I have worked for several major Division I coaches who put QUALITY attention into finding JuCo players. There are some coaches who specifically want to add one or two JuCo players to their roster each year and will scout them consistently.

Junior College players are important to NCAA programs that may have had many players transfer out, injuries or players who have exited school early for the draft. A team may be too heavy with a high percentage of freshman and incoming freshman on the roster and need a boost of older, more physically-ready players. Other programs may focus on Junior College players because they can't offer exciting locations or rankings—but they can offer players Division I starting jobs. JuCo players can come in to a program and make an immediate impact, the best ones are highly sought after by many elite BCS coaches.

More importantly, some Junior College players have been through their share of ups and downs and can be a more mature or goal-oriented than 17 or 18-year-old freshmen. JuCo players often appreciate the opportunity to play major college sports and are more disciplined than younger players. For many, this is their second chance and they are often more mature and willing to handle their business without being babysat compared to a player straight out of high school.

THE OBSTACLES THAT YOU FACE ARE STOPPING MOST OTHER PLAYERS TOO. WHEN YOU OVERCOME THEM, YOU TAKE A STEP AHEAD OF THE PACK TO SEPARATE YOURSELF!

Junior Colleges have helped pave the way to an NCAA career for many players, so consider it an option if you feel it's your best opportunity to lead you to a more competitive school than you are being recruited by as a high school senior. Visit www.NJCAA.org for more information!

Reach out to JuCo coaches in the same ways you would contact NCAA coaches—call, email, send your film, have your prep coaches call.

IF 'PLAN A' ISN'T WORKING OUT: WALK-ON OPPORTUNITIES

If you still dream of playing at the collegiate level and aren't getting scholarship offers or calls, evaluate if you would be able or willing to be a walk-on player. If your dream school has told you that they won't be able to offer you any scholarship money—would you be able to walk on? Is there a space for you and can you afford it?

30 TIPS FOR WALK-ONS: HOW TO MAKE THE TEAM AND TO EARN PLAYING TIME

BEFORE YOU MAKE THE TEAM

#1 – ASK HOW THE PROCESS WORKS: Walk-ons generally join the team in two ways, either as a preferred walk-on or through a tryout. A preferred walk-on doesn't have to tryout—they are borderline offers, favors for influential people or players from successful prep programs. Players that must tryout (MUST already be enrolled in classes at that university), complete compliance paperwork, get a physical and show up to the open tryout on a select date. You may need to weigh out your options after speaking with the schools that you are interested in to see which ones may be your best chance to make the team, it's not guaranteed and the spaces are extremely competitive. See how the process works at each school.

#2 – OTHER SCHOLARSHIPS AND LOANS: Apply for other scholarships (academic, service, legacy, major) and student loans. Nearly every other college student has to work to secure their scholarships and loans, so can you!

#3 - SEND HIGHLIGHT TAPE: Walk-on positions are just as competitive to get as scholarship spots, so you can approach the coaches in the same way—they need to see you play. Organize your highlight tape and your Student-Athlete Resume, contact the school, find out who the 'Walk-On Coordinator' is and forward your information to them for review. Follow-up within a week or two!

#4 - DO THEY NEED YOUR POSITION: Like scholarship spots, walk-on positions are usually slotted for a particular position or two that the team is lacking depth in. Again, if they are stacked at your position, they aren't likely to add you, choosing another player who can help at a position of need instead. Try back again in a year, and maybe even the next year.

#5 - WHAT ARE THEY LOOKING FOR: When you speak with the Walk-On Coordinator, ask them specifically what they are looking for—size, speed, grades, campus leadership? Each coach and program is looking to add something different—ask them specifically what type of players they need?

#6 - ASK FOR DRILLS: When you speak with the Walk-On Coordinator, ask them for drills, or ask your potential position coach for a few key drills. You can call or email for this information, or if you are already enrolled, stop by the office. It shows you are going above and beyond and willing to do the extra work to be prepared for your tryout. It won't guarantee you a spot (heck, you may not even get any sample drills), but it will show your work ethic and your desire to be prepared.

#7 - TRAIN: Prepare, prepare, prepare! Many players come out and haven't been putting in the consistent work that the current players have been putting in. Get up early and run, make strides in the weight room. Coaches are looking for skill, size and speed. Those are three ways you can get your foot in the door. Work on your position-specific drills, be in the best shape possible and train just as hard as the current scholarship athletes are training! Focus on improving skill, size and speed!

#8 - HAVE YOUR COACHES CALL: Ask your prep coaches to make a call to the coaches or Director of Operations to find out how the process works, what they are looking for and how you can secure a preferred walk-on spot or tryout. In some cases, your coach may be able to get more info that you can get.

#9 - ATTEND SUMMER CAMP: Entering your senior year of high school, if you haven't had much interest, particularly in your dream school, considering participating in their summer camp. It gives you a few days to network with the coaches and for them to get a chance to see you play. Coaches normally add a few players to their recruiting watch lists based off working with them in camp and after evaluating their size, skill and speed in person. You may not be scholarship-ready but you may be able to network with them and earn a walk-on spot. If you have a select school in mind, this is a great opportunity to get your foot in the door to try to earn a preferred walk-on slot. The earlier the better.

#10 – OFFER TO WORK CAMPS: If you are already enrolled at the university, check with the Camp Director or the Director of Operations in the spring and submit a resume or letter of interest, offering to work summer camps. These part-time positions may be on a week-by-week basis or may last throughout several weeks during the summer. Although they often pay, be willing to negotiate to volunteer if there are no extra positions available. Anything you can do to get your foot in the door, networking with the coaches and decision-makers, will give them a chance to see your work ethic and passion. You may be coaching elementary students or filling up the Gatorade coolers, but this can be an audition to show the coaches how hard you are willing to work to be a part of the program and get inside information on what skills they are looking for, what drills you can be working on and what sizes/speeds coaches are looking to bring in. Again, you might not make the team on the first try but at least they'll be able to put a name with a face and that always helps.

#11 – MULTIPLE TRY-OUTS: If at first you don't succeed, try... try again! I've been a part of many teams where a player eventually made the squad after trying out more than one time. If you don't make the cut the first year (don't play a position of need, aren't big or fast enough) then use that year to keep training. It is not uncommon for players to have to try out more than once to be able to make the team. Humble yourself and keep showing up!

#12 – STUDENT MANAGER: A similar idea to working camps. Any way you can get your foot in the door, networking with the coaches, understanding what they are looking for, seeing first-hand how hard the players work and what drills they participate in will only help you. It's not uncommon for a walk-on to make the team after working for a year or two as a manager. If you work hard, are willing to do anything to help the team (laundry, class checks, field set-up) on that level, coaches will take your work ethic into consideration as they are making their decisions. You will have an edge over other candidates who they have no relationship with.

#13 – ACADEMICS COUNT: Most walk-ons have outstanding grades, and their academic standing can help boost the team's overall GPA and academic standing. Coaches sometimes have enough trouble monitoring their scholarship players and their grades, they will not tolerate a walk-on player who isn't pulling their weight in the classroom. Don't let your academic standing be a reason to eliminate you from consideration, coaches are looking to add scholars and leaders, not just average students!

#14 – HOW CAN YOU BRING VALUE TO THE TEAM: Similar to scholarship players, what can you do to separate yourself and bring value to the team? Are you a top scholar, a student leader, a special teams superstar, an undersized speedster, someone who will take scout team extremely seriously? Can you be the best rebounder on the court? Find a way to get an edge—through leadership, academics, toughness or attitude. What is the team lacking, how can you become a specialist at that skill?

#15 – LOCAL PRODUCT: If playing for your hometown team is your dream, guess what—you actually have a slight advantage over other potential walk-ons. Coaches LOVE adding a local player or two who was a great hometown player in the area who may be choosing to stay closer to home, who is a life-long fan and who has local following. Contact the coaches or have your prep coach contact the Walk-On Coordinator during your junior or senior year and get the conversation going! Coaches are likely open to it, especially if you were a great player and leader for your high school!

YOU MAKE THE TEAM, HOW TO EARN PLAYING TIME:

#16 – PLAYBOOK, FILM JUNKIE: Earn the respect of your coaches and teammates by knowing the playbook better than any other player and by becoming a filmroom junkie. Although you may not be as naturally talented as other scholarship players, understanding the playbook backwards and forwards can only help you, and can help you assist your coaches and teammates during games. Many walk-ons become future coaches, and that begins with learning the importance of having a high IQ in your sport in terms of strategy, core philosophy and personnel. Being one of the smartest and most prepared players in the meeting room will help you get on the field at some point. Film will also give you an advantage, so once you understand how to get the most of it and you will be able to anticipate plays better in live games, you may pick up on tendencies quickly and be able to communicate those to your coaches or teammates. This can be one of your best angles to get some playing time!

#17 – MAKE TEAMMATES BETTER: Be serious in meetings and during practice on scout team, do whatever you can do to make your teammates better. Don't be frustrated as a player on scout team, take great pride in it, it IS your way to help the team! The more prepared they are, the more reps they are able to get in during practice, the more successful they are likely to be. Initiate extra reps after practice with your teammates, offer to help, stay late or come in on off days to help the starters! You will be improving as well and getting a step closer to some playing time!

#18 – FIRST THERE, LAST TO LEAVE: Coaches appreciate players who are ready to come to work every day. A key way to earn respect is by being the first player there and the last player to leave. Get in extra reps for yourself, or as mentioned above, help make the starters better by initiating extra reps after practice or on off days. Coaches will take notice! Those 15 or 30 extra minutes of drills will add up over the season and you will become a better player. Ask your coach for drills that you need work on and can do on your own, they love nothing more than players who take initiative to get better!

#19 – WAIT FOR CHANCE: A lot of walk-ons may go into the process thinking that playing time in-game is your chance. That's going to be a goal you will work towards down the road. Realize that scout team IS your chance. The role of scout team is very important to coaches, and can make a difference in the success of the team. Take pride and ownership of your unit, just as you would of your position group if you were a starter. Keep it competitive versus first and second teamers. Play fundamentally sound, if coaches can trust you in practice to not make careless mistakes they'll be more likely to trust you in game situations! Your first goal is to be the most outstanding scout team player and getting playing time in that way. Many walk-ons may not even see practice time, let alone game time. Realize that this is your first goal! The better you do preparing the team through scout team, the more likely your coaches will trust you in live game situations down the road!

#20 – DO WHATEVER YOU CAN TO MAKE A DIFFERENCE: A lot of walk-ons join the team trying to be 'too cool.' They are sometimes bigger divas than the top recruits. Humble yourself, keep a positive attitude and do whatever you can do for your teammates and coaches to be able to make a difference. Drop the diva attitude, a humble attitude will get you much, much further!

#21 – CONSISTENT AND DEPENDABLE: Another thing coaches are looking for are players who are consistent and dependable—in everything that they do. In your unit, if you can be the player who provides consistency, stability and reliability to the team, you will earn your coaches respect. Take it a step further, once you are part of the team and hanging out with the other players outside of the facility, be the voice of reason in situations where starters and scholarship players may need guidance. If you are around negative situations or altercations, help remove the starters and scholarship players from the environment—never be the one who escalates it. You will be off the roster immediately, be the 'voice of reason' when your coaches aren't around.

#22 – DO THE DIRTY WORK: Special teams, rebounding, blocking, toughness, extra work.... Again, everyone wants to be the leading scorer, rusher, playmaker but there are key skills that COACHES are looking for that can help win games. They may not get the glory or the fans, but they are critical skills in helping the team win. Do those tasks that most other players think they are too good for—

blocking, rebounding, cheerleading from the bench, running scout team. Get in there and get your jersey dirty. Make a difference in those skills that actually help change the game.

#23 – THERE FOR THE RIGHT REASONS: A key piece of advice that I give elite scholarship athletes is "Chase greatness and everything else will come." This applies to walk-ons as well. Over the years I've noticed that a good percentage of walk-ons are 'in it' for the wrong reasons, they aren't necessarily there for the love of the game. Those players never last or see playing time, the walk-ons who are eventually put in a position to earn playing time are the ones who are chasing GREATNESS first—not the opposite sex, media, popularity or any of the other fringe benefits. Be there for the right reason—the love of the game and your school—and you'll succeed!

#24 – BIGGEST CHEERLEADER: It cannot be stated enough how important ENERGY and MOMENTUM can help your team. As a walk-on, you may not see much playing time but you do play a major role during competitions. Clap it up—when things are going good, when the team is facing sudden change or adversity or when the game is on the line. Even when a key player makes a critical mistake, be the first one over to tell them to keep their head up and that they'll make the play next time. Keep your teammates confident and focused and bring the energy to the sideline! In and out of quarters or halftime, between time-outs—CLAP IT UP! That is your job, and YES, it can help win!

#25 – DON'T HARASS STAFF: Many walk-ons are some of the most popular and fun players on the team, they're happy to be there. Other walk-ons think they have to be DEMANDING in order to earn respect. I've come across my fair share of walk-ons who always tried to demand extra equipment, gear, exceptions and it's something coaches don't want to hear about. Treat your academic counselors, equipment managers, trainers and other staff with respect or you could find yourself cut from the roster for having a disrespecting attitude. You can't demand respect, go earn it.

#26 – MENTOR YOUNGER PLAYERS: Once you are on the team and a veteran, take some of the freshmen under your wing, especially at your position. Coaches are always looking for leaders within the team, and you will be helping your position out if you can help mentor a rookie and show them the ropes, on and off-campus. Tips for class, laundry, cooking, rides, breaking the ice...

#27 – HELP WITH RECRUITING: On official visit weekends, recruits are paired up with hosts, and there are some occasions where coaches would pair up a player with a walk-on, they are at times the funniest or most personable players on the team. They may actually have more passion or school spirit, and it can be infectious! Anything you can do to help the team, including hosting a prospect or helping during official visit weekends will be a help to your coaches.

#28 – PARENTS: Coaches don't usually respond well when parents call to complain about playing time or petty stuff. They ESPECIALLY don't like it if it's for a walk-on, particularly if you aren't a key scout team or special teams player. In my experience, we once had a parent who constantly complained that their walk-on son should be starting ahead of the current starter... a player who would go on to win multiple Super Bowl Championships as a starter. Appreciate your opportunity and keep the complaints about playing time to a minimum. Champions never complain their way out of a problem, they work their way out!

#29 – NEVER EMBARRASS THE TEAM OR THE COACHES: Especially in the newspapers—arrests or incidents with the police will be another quick way to find yourself off the team. Again, you may not even have the opportunity to give the coaches your side of the story if there is a pattern of bad behavior or legal incidents. Some coaches tolerate legal issues with scholarship players and may give them second or third chances but most won't tolerate issues with walk-ons. You are there to bring positive light to the program, never negative attention!

#30 – HAVE FUN: Most importantly, HAVE FUN! Playing at the collegiate level, in the sport that you love, will be a life-changing experience. To many walk-ons, it's an experience they'd actually pay for at the end of the day. I'd give up many things to go back to those four seasons in undergrad with my team! If every other regular student has to find scholarships or loans or depend on their family, then you are simply doing the same thing and getting the chance to live out your dream—being part of your college team! Enjoy it!

IF 'PLAN A' ISN'T WORKING OUT: ISSUES WITH THE NCAA

The NCAA and their rules and member institutions make up a very complex and powerful world. As you are submitting information to the NCAA Eligibility Center and working towards admission and enrollment to your chosen university you may encounter setbacks. You may have academic credit deficiencies, questions and investigations into your amateur status, flagged SAT/ACT scores, problems with your transcripts... the NCAA problems that players can run into are limitless.

The #1 rule to remember during this time is to just be honest, tell the truth. If the NCAA catches you in a lie, your shot is over. They take their time, attempt to get all of the information and rarely rush to a decision. It's best to take a deep breath, tell the truth and wait out a decision. Even if you are guilty on some level and tell the truth, you may face reinstatement or minor punishments. If you are guilty and lie about it, they are doing their investigations interviewing several other people involved in the situation and can permanently end your career if they come to the conclusion that you are lying.

I've worked with a handful of players and coaches who were in the center of NCAA investigations—some minor and some that became national news. In high profile cases, the public perception is that players and coaches are guilty until proven innocent. It's not fair, but it is the case. That's why it's best to be honest, keep a low profile and wait on the investigation to run its course.

IF 'PLAN A' ISN'T WORKING OUT: WHAT IF AN INJURY INTERRUPTS MY CAREER

One of the toughest adversities all athletes face are injuries, particularly season or career-ending injuries. From my experiences, they are much tougher mentally on most players than physically.

From a recruiting standpoint, not all season-ending injuries will effect your potential to earn a scholarship. From my experiences, college coaches will often stick by injured players and continue to recruit and evaluate them, possibly even offer them. If you already have scholarship offers, an injury doesn't necessarily mean that they will be pulled.

The toughest situation is for those players who are seniors and still working towards getting offers, if you find yourself in this situation you will just need to get more creative and more aggressive. The key to success in this situation is to remain mentally tough. You must keep your confidence, develop other aspects of your game, become a master of the playbook.

If you are a basketball player who breaks their leg—get in the job, get someone to help rebound for you, and get shots up! If you break your right hand, get in the gym and learn to shoot with your left hand, work on your quickness, vertical and conditioning.

If you are an unsigned senior, you must continue to pound the pavement, work the phones, send your highlights and follow-up. You may have to go to prep school, Junior College or a much less competitive program.

You must find a way to OVERCOME. You must work towards this every day. You must stay positive! Remember—you always have options, even if you may not see them in the moment.

AS YOU DEVELOP PHYSICALLY INTO A GREAT PLAYER, YOU MUST DEVELOP MENTALLY AS WELL. YOU MUST TRAIN YOURSELF TO TUNE OUT CRITICISM AND TO WORK THROUGH THE SLUMPS.

WHAT TO EXPECT IN HIGH SCHOOL... FROM FRESHMAN TO SENIOR YEAR

"Fear of failure leads to failure."
– PAULO COELHO

"The trouble with most of us is that we would rather be ruined by praise than saved by criticism."
– NORMAN VINCENT PEALE

"Worry does not empty tomorrow of its sorrow; it empties today of its strength."
– CORRIE TEN BROOM

WHAT TO EXPECT:
FRESHMAN YEAR OF HS

:: FOCUS ON FUNDAMENTALS... within your sport and become a master of those! Don't worry about the recruiting process; focus all of your energy on being the best player that you can be and on being a great leader and teammate. The better you play, the better your odds are of being discovered! Put 100% effort into your fundamentals—even if you are on the JV or Freshman team!

IF YOU WANT MORE SUCCESS, SURROUND YOURSELF WITH THOSE THAT HAVE SUCCESS. IF YOU WANT DRAMA, SURROUND YOURSELF WITH DRAMA!

:: PLAY HARD... Nearly every school in nearly every sport relies on regional or national scouting services. Universities pay an annual fee for reports from established scouts, especially for information on top freshmen and sophomores. Each service normally provides contact info and a short 10-word-or-less description of the athletes' style of play, and ranks them with a letter or category grade (Division I, II, III, NAIA). These reports are scanned for sizes, speeds, stats and notes from observations. Be aware that there are eyes everywhere—not just the college coaches themselves! (LOW/MID/HIGH LEVEL PLAYERS)

:: FOCUS ON YOUR GRADES... and set good study habits. Set aside time for homework each day. Your freshman and sophomore grades will be heavily evaluated when you are a junior. Get off to a great start.

:: MAKE SURE YOUR GRADES EXCEED THE 'NCAA SLIDING SCALE' STANDARDS – Division I signees need to qualify academically based on their Core GPA and ACT/SAT test scores. Division II requires even higher SAT/ACT minimums. Even if you dream is to go Division I, have the grades to qualify for Division II as well, you don't want to miss out on additional scholarship opportunities. Additionally, each university sets their own academic standards which may be even higher than the NCAA Division I or Division II standards.

FRESHMAN YEAR, GET AHEAD BY...

:: ATTENDING SUMMER CAMPS OR CLINICS... at the schools that you are interested in and combines managed by third-parties (AAU, Nike, etc). Any regional or national tournaments or exposure events you can attend will be helpful. By attending as a younger player you can get over the anxiousness and uncertainty of the drills and be more polished as an upperclassman.

:: IF SENT A QUESTIONNAIRE BY A SCHOOL... fill it out and return it promptly! It is a sign of interest, RESPOND!

WHAT TO EXPECT:
SOPHOMORE YEAR OF HS

:: FOCUS ON FUNDAMENTALS... within your sport and become a master of those! Don't worry about the recruiting process; focus all of your energy on being the best player that you can be and on being a great leader and teammate. The better you play and the more games your team wins, the better your odds are of being discovered! Put 100% effort into your fundamentals—even if you are on the JV team!

:: FOCUS ON YOUR GRADES... and set good study habits. Set aside time for homework each day. Your sophomore grades will be heavily evaluated when you are a junior. You don't want grades to be a factor that eliminates you off of a coach's 'watch list' later down the road.

:: MAKE SURE YOUR GRADES EXCEED THE 'NCAA SLIDING SCALE' STANDARDS – Division I signees need to qualify academically based on their Core GPA and ACT/SAT test scores. Division II requires even higher SAT/ACT minimums. Even if you dream is to go Division I, have the grades to qualify for Division II as well, you don't want to miss out on all of those additional scholarship opportunities. Additionally, each university sets their own student-athlete academic standards which may be even higher than the NCAA Division I or Division II standards.

STOP LETTING THE LITTLE NEGATIVE THINGS KEEP YOU FROM THE BIG, POSITIVE STEPS YOU NEED TO TAKE.

:: IF SENT A QUESTIONNAIRE BY A SCHOOL... fill it out and return it promptly! It is a sign of interest, RESPOND!

:: AFTER YOUR SOPHOMORE SEASON IT IS A GOOD IDEA TO BEGIN TO TAKE THE ACT OR SAT TEST... By testing early, it will give you an idea of what subjects you need to make improvements in during the next few years. Check with your coach or guidance counselor, there are NCAA standards (and different standards at each university) that must be met with your GPA and your ACT/SAT test scores. If you are financially unable to afford the ACT/SAT tests, check with your coach or guidance counselor for a financial wavier! Most schools REQUIRE a copy of your ACT/SAT/PSAT scores before allowing you to make an official visit.

:: **PLAY HARD...** As a sophomore, you are too young to contact but coaches may begin doing their homework on you if you are a top player in the area. It is still very early in the process, but some college staffs work ahead by beginning their research on recruiting classes a couple years in advance. Coaches may call around to find out more about your talent level, how you compete vs. local players and if there are red flags concerning your character or academic standing as early as your sophomore year.

Nearly every school in nearly every sport relies on regional or national scouting services. Universities pay an annual fee for reports from established scouts, especially for information on top freshmen and sophomores. Each service normally provides contact info and a short 10-word-or-less description of the athletes' style of play, and ranks them with a letter or category grade (Division I, II, III, NAIA). These reports are scanned for sizes, speeds, stats and notes from observations. Be aware that there are eyes everywhere—not just the college coaches themselves! (LOW/MID/HIGH LEVEL PLAYERS)

Coaches will begin noting top underclassmen to add to the database for future recruitment as they attend practices or tournaments. Be aware that they are watching and making notes, even if they aren't able to contact you. (HIGH/MID/LOW LEVEL players)

Coaches will begin screening highlight tape, stats, regional all-star teams and rankings for top regional players and may add underclassmen names to their watch lists for future recruitment. (HIGH INTEREST)

:: **INVITE YOU TO CAMPUS...** If you are an elite player in the area, coaches may be inviting your team to their summer camps or sports clinics as a sophomore. If financially possible, attend those at the universities you are interested in! Camps can be a very important step in the process for both the prospect and the coaching staff. (HIGH LEVEL)

As a prospect, they are able to offer you complimentary admission (via a pass list at the gate) for you and up to two guests. (MEDIUM/HIGH INTEREST)

SOPHOMORE YEAR, GET AHEAD BY ...

:: **ATTEND SUMMER CAMPS OR CLINICS...** at the schools that you are interested in and combines managed by third-parties (AAU, Nike, etc). Any regional or national tournaments or exposure events you can attend will be helpful. By attending as a younger player you can get over the anxiousness and uncertainty of the drills and be more polished as an upperclassman.

:: **BEING ACADEMICALLY ON TRACK...** Sit down with your guidance counselor to make sure your course load is in line with NCAA (Division I and II standards) and university requirements. If you are aiming to attend an academically prestigious university, see what their typical freshman academic profile is. Yes, some schools are able to make exceptions in admissions for student-athletes, but many have a limited number of spots for the entire athletic department to use. Many universities do not have much wiggle room academically between the general student population and student-athletes. Be prepared!

WHAT TO EXPECT:
JUNIOR YEAR OF HS

:: **FOCUS ON FUNDAMENTALS...** within your sport and become a master of those! Don't waste time worrying about the recruiting process, focus all of your energy on being the best player that you can be. If you are a top player, make sure you work on becoming a great leader and teammate—these are qualities coaches are looking for in addition to size and skill! The better you play and the more games your team wins, the better your odds are of being discovered! Put 100% effort into your fundamentals!

:: **IF SENT A QUESTIONNAIRE BY THE SCHOOL...** fill it out and return it promptly! It is a sign of interest, RESPOND!

:: **BE ON TRACK ACADEMICALLY...** Sit down with your guidance counselor to make sure your course load is in line with NCAA (Division I and Division II) and university requirements. If you are aiming to attend an academically prestigious university, see what their typical freshman academic profile is. Yes, some schools are able to make exceptions in admissions for student-athletes, but many have a limited number of spots for the entire athletic department to use. Many universities do not have much wiggle room academically between the general student population and student-athletes. Be prepared!

:: **MAKE ARRANGEMENTS TO TAKE THE ACT OR SAT TEST – it is MANDATORY!** Check with your coach or guidance counselor, there are NCAA standards (and different standards at each university) that must be met with your GPA and your ACT/SAT test scores. If you are financially unable to afford the ACT/SAT tests, check with your coach or guidance counselor for a financial wavier! Most schools REQUIRE a copy of your ACT/SAT/PSAT scores before allowing you to make an official visit.

:: MAKE SURE YOUR GRADES EXCEED THE 'NCAA SLIDING SCALE' STANDARDS – Division I signees need to qualify academically based on their Core GPA and ACT/SAT test scores. Division II requires even higher SAT/ACT minimums. Even if you dream is to go Division I, have the grades to qualify for Division II as well, you don't want to miss out on all of those additional scholarship opportunities. Additionally, each university sets their own student-athlete academic standards which may be even higher than the NCAA Division I or Division II standards.

:: REGISTER FOR THE NCAA CLEARINGHOUSE - All prospective student-athletes MUST register with the NCAA Eligibility Center (www.EligibilityCenter.org) in order to practice, play and receive a Division I or Division II athletic scholarship. The NCAA Eligibility Center oversees the certification process to confirm academic credentials and amateurism status. The NCAA Eligibility Center determines if players are ruled eligible, and able to compete and accept a scholarship. High school students can register with the NCAA Eligibility Center at any time but it is recommended that you begin the process during your junior year. Prospective student-athletes must submit transcripts from all schools attended, report SAT/ACT scores directly from the testing agency (use code 9999 when registering for the tests to have your scores sent) and submit the $70 fee. The Eligibility Center confirms that #1- you have graduated, #2- have completed the required number of core courses (varies depending on Division I or II and graduation year), #3- earned a minimum GPA, #4- earned a qualifying SAT/ACT score and #5- completed an amateurism questionnaire and #6- have requested final amateurism certification.

:: ATTEND SUMMER CAMPS OR CLINICS... at schools that you are interested in and combines managed by third-parties (AAU, Nike, etc). Any regional or national tournaments or exposure events you can attend will be helpful.

SACRIFICES ARE NOT PUNISHMENTS, THEY ARE INVESTMENTS! INVEST BIG TO WIN BIG, YOU HAVE TO SACRIFICE CONSISTENTLY!

:: YOU MAY BEGIN RECEIVING MAIL... cards, letters, emails and information on the university and program. If you begin to receive this information from schools it means you are on their watch list and they need more information on you and to see you play, either in person or on tape before they can determine if you are a candidate for a scholarship. The date when schools may begin contacting you varies by sport, check NCAA.org for more info. (Low-High Interest From Coaches)

:: **IN-PERSON VISITS...** If you are a priority recruit, coaches will come to your school as NCAA periods allow – they will watch practice, meet with your coach and show their face around school to let you know they're interested. As a junior, a college coach may not make in-person contact (speak) with you off their campus but may make academic or athletic evaluations. [MEDIUM/HIGH Interest From Coach]

:: **REQUEST TRANSCRIPT...** If interested, coaches may request a copy of your transcript from your coach or guidance counselor to determine if you would be able to pass their academic standards (university and athletic department standards). Coaches are actively recruiting several players and don't want to waste a lot of time if they know you would not be able to get admitted into their university or fit their basic standards. Many athletic departments have academic advisors who evaluate your current grades and make projections on how you will finish high school. They may recommend terminating your recruitment if they don't believe you can qualify or believe that you can be successful there. [MEDIUM/HIGH Interest From Coach]

:: **ASKING AROUND ABOUT YOU...** Coaches may call around to find out more about what your decision factors are, talent level, how you compete vs. local players and if there are red flags concerning your character or academic standing. They will call everyone to get a better picture of you as a player, student and person— your HS coaches, AAU coach, parents, prep coaches in your region or conference, guidance counselor, mentors, brothers, sisters or even other college coaches. [HIGH INTEREST]

:: **MONITORING YOUR SOCIAL MEDIA...** Coaches will likely be checking out your social media pages to find out more about you, what other schools you are visiting or being offered by and your thoughts on the process. Many coaches also use social media as the quickest way to communicate with you. Be aware they take into consideration your language, attitude and how you carry yourself. Nearly every coach I know has eliminated players from their watch list because of negativity from their Facebook or Twitter accounts. [HIGH INTEREST]

:: **EVALUATIONS & CONTACTS** – Each coach is allowed a set number of evaluations and contacts with each prospect per year, beginning the prospects junior year. If they are doing their homework on you or are interested, they will attend your games and practices and set up times to visit with your high school coach or guidance counselor. [Basic Definition - Evaluation: Any off-campus activity designed to assess the academic qualifications or athletics ability (during which no contact occurs) of a prospective student-athlete / Contact: Any face-to-face encounter between a prospective student-athlete or the prospective student-athlete's parents, relatives or legal guardians and an institutional staff member or athletics representative during which any dialogue occurs in excess of an exchange of a greeting.]- [HIGH INTEREST]

:: **GET YOU TO CAMPUS...** If coaches have developed some interest (not necessarily have made a decision to offer you a scholarship yet), they will try to get you to campus for an unofficial visit (expenses paid by prospect). Some unofficial visits are set up with individual players and are more personalized or others are Junior Days where hundreds of athletes are invited. They want to get to know you better, show you what they have to offer in terms of campus and facilities, give you an opportunity to get to know their players and introduce you to academic programs that you may be interested in. Recruiting is a two-way street so they are getting a read on your interest level and giving you an opportunity to get to know them better to see if they fit your needs. (MEDIUM/HIGH INTEREST)

Coaches may invite you to campus for games. As a prospect, they are able to offer you complimentary admission (via a pass list at the gate) for you and up to two guests. (MEDIUM/HIGH INTEREST)

:: **UNDERSTANDING YOUR INTEREST LEVEL...** Coaches will be asking you where else you have made unofficial visits to in order to gauge your interest level with their school. They may ask you what you liked or didn't like about the other schools you are looking at. If you are a rated player, most coaches learn about your unofficial visits on the internet so be prepared that they will ask you about your thoughts on the competition, you haven't done anything wrong—they just want to figure out your likes and dislikes and selection criteria. (HIGH INTEREST)

:: **INFORMATION ON MAJORS YOU ARE INTERESTED IN...** If coaches have a high interest in you, they may send you specific information on the academic major that interests you. They want to make sure you and your family know they are interested in you outside of just sports. (HIGH INTEREST)

:: **PLAY HARD...** Coaches will be evaluating highlight tapes, stats, regional all-star teams and rankings of juniors. This is a key year for you as a player! Following your junior season, send your highlight tape and Student-Athlete Resume (stats, measurements, accomplishments, awards, grades and contact information) to schools you are interested in via mail or email. (MEDIUM/HIGH INTEREST)

EVERY COLLEGE COACH THAT I KNOW SAY THEY'VE STOPPED RECRUITING A PLAYER BASED ON THEIR ONLINE STATUS UPDATES BECAUSE OF DISRESPECTFUL LANGUAGE

Nearly every school in nearly every sport relies on regional or national scouting services. Universities pay an annual fee for reports from established scouts. Each service normally provides contact info and a short 10-word-or-less description of the athletes' style of play, and ranks them with a letter or category grade (Division I, II, III, NAIA). These reports are scanned for sizes, speeds, stats and notes from observations and upperclassmen we may not have been aware of. Be aware that there are eyes everywhere—not just the college coaches themselves! (LOW/MID/HIGH LEVEL PLAYERS)

:: **SUMMER CAMPS...** If you are a recommended player or on their 'watch list,' coaches may be personally inviting you to their summer camps or sports clinics. If financially possible, attend those at the universities you are interested in! Camps can be a very important step in the process for both the prospect and the coaching staff. (LOW/MEDIUM/HIGH INTEREST)

:: **PHONE CALLS...** Depending on your sport, coaches may begin contacting you at some point during or after your junior year. If coaches have a high interest in you, they will likely be calling you the maximum number of times per week or month as allowed by the NCAA for your sport. The NCAA limits them in the number of times they are able to initiate phone calls with you, but you are able to call them as often as you would like. The dates when coaches may begin calling you and the frequency of calls varies by sport and is determined by the NCAA. Check NCAA.org for more info. (MEDIUM/HIGH INTEREST)

:: **IN-PERSON CONTACTS...** If you have been offered by a school and are a top priority for them, they will go out of their way to express their interest in you by showing up at your games and practices. There are times when coaches are making face-to-face contacts and in-person evaluations at your games to merely show support, understand that their time is very valuable and they are making a commitment to you by being present. (HIGH INTEREST)

:: **BUILDING RELATIONSHIPS...** Coaches understand that you are likely influenced (sometimes heavily) by your family, friends, coaches and mentors. Along with building a relationship with you, they are often building just as important relationships with those in your circle. If they are making this effort, understand you are a high priority to them. (HIGH INTEREST)

:: **COACHES MAY BE TRYING TO UNDERSTAND THE DYNAMICS WITHIN YOUR FAMILY** – if you are close-knit, have a need to stay close-to-home or if you are comfortable going away to school in another state. They are evaluating your family situation and the possibility of you realistically choosing their school. (HIGH INTEREST)

:: **IF YOU HAVE ACADEMIC, ATTITUDE OR CHARACTER RED-FLAGS...** coaches are constantly evaluating the risk-reward during recruitment. Are you worth the trouble based on your past actions, and are you making improvements in those areas and maturing? Are you worth the risk to them or are there other players just as talented who have zero red flags? (MEDIUM/HIGH INTEREST)

JUNIOR YEAR – GET AHEAD BY ...

:: START CONTACTING SCHOOLS ON YOUR OWN... If you haven't gotten much interest by the end of your junior year, you should start contacting schools on your own. Don't panic- you still have PLENTY of time! It is best to start with local or state schools (even if those aren't your first choice) and build interest instead of starting at the BCS Top 25 programs. Send your highlights, stats, awards, accomplishments and contact information to schools within an hour or two and follow-up within a week with someone personally on the phone. Find out which coach on staff recruits your geographic region or position—your overall goal is to get your highlight tape in their hands and to get them to watch it and give you feedback. Since most schools first question to you will be "Who have you been offered by?" – it is easier to begin generating interest or offers from local or smaller schools than by contacting national Top 25 teams.

:: SET UP UNOFFICIAL VISITS AFTER YOUR SEASON... If you fit the athletic standards of a school, your junior year is a good time to take as many unofficial visits as possible to the schools that you are seriously interested in. Financially, it may not be an option but if it is, the only way to really decide if you like a school or program is to visit it in person. In several regions, you are able to visit many universities and colleges within a manageable drive. The quantity of schools that you visit isn't important, but rather the quality of programs that fit your needs and skill level. You may not like them in person or your interest may double or triple after making a visit. Definitely get in touch with the recruiting coach before your visit and tell them you would like to check out the campus and try to set up a meeting in advance if possible.

WHAT TO EXPECT:
SENIOR YEAR OF HS

:: FOCUS ON FUNDAMENTALS... within your sport and become a master of those! Focus your energy on being the best player that you can be. Coaches at every program are looking for great players. It's never too late, even after Signing Day, there are still opportunities. If you are a top player, make sure you work on becoming a great leader and teammate—these are qualities that coaches are looking for in addition to size and skill! The better you play and the more games your team wins, the better your odds are of being discovered! Put 100% effort into your fundamentals!

:: IF SENT A QUESTIONNAIRE BY A SCHOOL... fill it out and return it promptly! It is a sign of interest, RESPOND!

:: **MAKE ARRANGEMENTS TO TAKE THE ACT OR SAT TEST – it is MANDATORY!**
Check with your coach or guidance counselor, there are NCAA standards (and different standards at each university) that must be met with your GPA and your ACT/SAT test scores. If you are financially unable to afford the ACT/SAT tests, check with your coach or guidance counselor for a financial wavier! Most schools REQUIRE a copy of your ACT/SAT/PSAT scores before allowing you to make an official visit.

:: **MAKE SURE YOUR GRADES EXCEED THE 'NCAA SLIDING SCALE' STANDARDS**
– Division I signees need to qualify academically based on their Core GPA and ACT/SAT test scores. Division II requires even higher SAT/ACT minimums. Even if you dream is to go Division I, have the grades to qualify for Division II as well, you don't want to miss out on all of those additional scholarship opportunities. Additionally, each university sets their own student-athlete academic standards which may be even higher than the NCAA Division I or Division II standards.

:: **ATTEND SUMMER CAMPS OR CLINICS...** at the schools you are interested in and combines managed by third-parties (AAU, Nike, etc). Any regional or national tournaments or exposure events you can attend will be helpful.

:: **REGISTER FOR THE NCAA CLEARINGHOUSE** - All prospective student-athletes MUST register with the NCAA Eligibility Center (www.EligibilityCenter.org) in order to practice, play and receive a Division I or Division II athletic scholarship. The NCAA Eligibility Center oversees the certification process to confirm academic credentials and amateurism status. The NCAA Eligibility Center determines if players are ruled eligible, and able to compete and accept a scholarship. High school students can register with the NCAA Eligibility Center at any time but it is recommended that you begin the process during your junior year. Prospective student-athletes must submit transcripts from all schools attended, report SAT/ACT scores directly from the testing agency (use code 9999 when registering for the tests to have your scores sent) and submit the $70 fee. The Eligibility Center confirms that #1- you have graduated, #2- have completed the required number of core courses (varies depending on Division I or II and graduation year), #3- earned a minimum GPA, #4- earned a qualifying SAT/ACT score and #5- completed an amateurism questionnaire and #6- have requested final amateurism certification.

:: **YOU MAY BEGIN RECEIVING MAIL...** cards, letters, emails and information on the university and program. If you begin to receive this information from schools it means you are on their watch list and they need more information on you and to see you play, either in person or on tape before they can determine if you are a candidate for a scholarship. (Low-High Interest From Coaches)

If you fit the athletic standards of a school, the summer before your senior year is a good time to take as many unofficial visits as possible to the schools that you are seriously interested in. [Note: In men's and women's basketball, there are restrictions for unofficial visits during July, check with the NCAA or each university before planning a trip.] Financially, it may not be an option but if it is, the only way to really decide if you like a school or program is to visit it in person. In several regions, you are able to visit many universities and colleges within a manageable drive. The quantity of schools that you visit isn't important, but rather the quality of programs that fit your needs. You may not like them in person or your interest may double or triple after making a visit. If you haven't been in contact with a member of the coaching staff yet but are interested, contact the school first and ask for the coach who recruits your geographic area. Get in touch with the recruiting coach before your visit and tell them you would like to check out the campus and try to set up a meeting in advance if possible.

:: IN-PERSON VISITS... If you are a priority recruit, coaches will come to your school as NCAA periods allow – they will watch practice, meet with your coach, show their face around school to let you know they're interested. Depending on the team of year they may not be able to contact (speak to you in-person) but can evaluate your academic and athletic abilities. (MEDIUM/HIGH Interest From Coach)

:: REQUEST TRANSCRIPT... If interested, coaches may request a copy of your transcript from your coach or guidance counselor to determine if you would be able to pass their academic standards (university and athletic department standards). Coaches are actively recruiting several players and don't want to waste a lot of time if they know you would not be able to get admitted into their university or fit their basic standards. Many athletic departments have academic advisors who evaluate your current grades and make projections on how you will finish high school. They may recommend terminating your recruitment if they don't believe you can be successful there. (MEDIUM/HIGH Interest From Coach)

:: ASKING AROUND ABOUT YOU... Coaches will call around to find out more about what your decision factors are, talent level, how you compete vs. local players and if there are red flags concerning your character or academic standing. They will call everyone to get a better picture of you as a player, student and person—your HS coaches, AAU coach, parents, prep coaches in your region or conference, guidance counselor, mentors, brothers, sisters or even other college coaches. (HIGH INTEREST)

:: MONITORING YOUR SOCIAL MEDIA... Coaches will likely be checking out your social media pages to find out more about you, what other schools you are visiting or being offered by and your thoughts on the process. Many coaches also use social media as the quickest way to communicate with you. Be aware they take into consideration your language, attitude and how you carry yourself. Nearly every coach I know has eliminated players from their list because of negativity from their Facebook or Twitter accounts. (HIGH INTEREST)

:: **EVALUATIONS & CONTACTS** – Each coach is allowed a set number of evaluations and contacts with each prospect per year, beginning the prospects junior year. If they are doing their homework on you or interested, they will attend your games and practices and set up times to visit with your high school coach or guidance counselor. [Basic Definition - Evaluation: Any off-campus activity designed to assess the academic qualifications or athletics ability (during which no contact occurs) of a prospective student-athlete / Contact: Any face-to-face encounter between a prospective student-athlete or the prospective student-athlete's parents, relatives or legal guardians and an institutional staff member or athletics representative during which any dialogue occurs in excess of an exchange of a greeting.] [HIGH INTEREST]

:: **SET UP IN-HOME VISIT...** If a coach has offered you and is hoping you will commit to their school, they will set up an in-home visit with your family. Each school is allowed only one in-home visit per prospective student-athlete. [HIGH INTEREST]

:: **SET UP OFFICIAL VISIT...** If coaches have offered you a scholarship, they will try to get you (and likely your family) to set up a date to make an official visit (expenses for prospect paid by school) to campus. Prospects are only able to visit up to five schools on official visits, and they may last up to a maximum of 48 hours. Some prospects come alone and others are joined by their extended family. [HIGH INTEREST]

:: **INFORMATION ON MAJORS YOU ARE INTERESTED IN...** If coaches have a high interest in you, they may send you specific information on the academic major that interests you. They want to make sure you and your family knows that they are interested in you beyond just sports. [HIGH INTEREST]

:: **INVITE YOU TO CAMPUS...** If there is a medium to high level of interest, coaches will invite you to campus for games. As a prospect, they are able to offer you complimentary admission (via a pass list at the gate) for you and up to two guests. [MEDIUM/HIGH INTEREST]

If you are a recommended player or on their 'watch list,' coaches may be personally inviting you to their summer camps or sports clinics. If financially possible, attend those at the universities you are interested in! Camps can be a very important step in the process for both the prospect and the coaching staff. [MEDIUM/HIGH INTEREST]

BE HUMBLE OR
BE HUMBLED!

If coaches have developed some interest (not necessarily have made a decision to offer you a scholarship), they will try to get you to campus for an unofficial visit (expenses paid by prospect).

Some unofficial visits are schedule with individual players and are more personalized or others are open to hundreds of athletes and are much more informal. They want to get to know you better, show you what they have to offer in terms of campus and facilities, give you an opportunity to get to know their players and introduce you to academic programs you may be interested in. Recruiting is a two-way street so they are getting a read on your interest level and giving you an opportunity to get to know them better to see if they fit your needs. [MEDIUM/HIGH INTEREST]

:: PLAY HARD... Coaches will still be evaluating highlight tapes, stats, regional all-star teams and rankings of seniors. There is still time to pick up interests and offers from plenty of universities. During or immediately following your senior season, send your highlight tape and/or stats, measurements, accomplishments, awards, grades and contact information to schools you are interested in via mail or email. Follow-up with each university that you are interested in and try to get a coach or recruiting coordinator on the phone to determine if they are interested or not.

Nearly every school in nearly every sport relies on regional or national scouting services. Universities pay an annual fee for reports from established scouts, especially for information on top freshmen and sophomores. Each service normally provides contact info and a short 10-word-or-less description of the athletes' style of play, and ranks them with a letter or category grade (Division I, II, III, NAIA). These reports are scanned for sizes, speeds, stats and notes from observations. Be aware that there are eyes everywhere—not just the college coaches themselves! [LOW/MID/HIGH LEVEL PLAYERS]

:: PHONE CALLS... If coaches have a high interest in you, they will likely be calling you the maximum number of times per week or month as allowed by the NCAA for your sport. The NCAA limits them in the number of times they are able to initiate phone calls with you, but you are able to call them as often as you would like. The dates when coaches may begin calling you and the frequency of calls varies by sport and is determined by the NCAA. [MEDIUM/HIGH INTEREST]

:: IN-PERSON CONTACTS... If you have been offered by a school and are a top priority for them, they will go out of their way to express their interest in you by showing up at your games and practices. There are times when coaches are making face-to-face contacts and in-person evaluations at your games to merely show support, understand that their time is very valuable and they are making a commitment to you by being present. [HIGH INTEREST]

:: BUILDING RELATIONSHIPS... Coaches understand that you are likely influenced (sometimes heavily) by your family, friends, coaches and mentors. Along with building a relationship with you, they are often building just as important relationships with those in your circle. If they are making this effort, understand you are a priority to them. (HIGH INTEREST)

If you are a priority recruit, coaches are getting to understand the dynamics within your family – if you are close-knit, have a need to stay close-to-home or if you are comfortable going away to school in another state. They are evaluating your family situation and the possibility of you realistically choosing their school. (HIGH INTEREST)

:: IF YOU HAVE ACADEMIC, ATTITUDE OR CHARACTER RED-FLAGS... Coaches are always evaluating the risk-reward of your recruitment. Are you worth the trouble based on your past actions, and are you making improvements in those areas and maturing? Are you worth the risk to them or are there other players just as talented who have zero red flags? (MEDIUM/HIGH INTEREST)

AS A SENIOR, YOU STILL CAN...

:: START CONTACTING SCHOOLS ON YOUR OWN... If you haven't gotten much interest by the beginning or end of your senior season, you should start contacting schools on your own. Don't panic- you still have time. It is best to start with local or state schools (even if those aren't your first choice) and build interest instead of starting at the BSC Top 25 programs. Send your highlight tapes, stats, awards, accomplishments and contact information to schools within an hour or two and follow-up within a few weeks with someone personally on the phone. Find out which coach on staff recruits your geographic region or position—your overall goal is to get your highlight tape in their hands and to get them to watch it and give you feedback. Since most schools first question to you will be "Who have you been offered by?" – it is easier to begin generating interest or offers from local schools than by contacting the defending national champions or elite national teams.

FRUSTRATION MAKES YOU WANT TO QUIT. THE KEY IS TO PUSH PAST THAT LAYER AND WANT TO DO BETTER

CHAPTER #9

WHAT SEPARATES GOOD PLAYERS FROM GREAT ONES: LEADERSHIP, SACRIFICES AND TIME MANAGEMENT

"Don't be distracted by criticism. The only taste of success that some people have is when they take a bite out of you."
– ZIG ZIGLAR

"He who sacrifices most wins."

"Your life does not get better by chance, it gets better by change."
– JIM ROHN

25 TIPS TO BECOME A BETTER LEADER

#1- Don't blame anyone, ever. If times get tough, put the team on your back and say, "I should/could have done more." And understand and believe in that statement – you can always lead everyone to do more. Never throw your teammates or coaches under the bus. Even if they probably deserve it, your reactions will only make the situation worse. If necessarily, pull them aside one-on-one.

#2- Realize that it's up to you. If you are a junior or a senior- you NEED to become a leader. If you are one of the most talented players on the team, you NEED to be a leader. The lockerroom is waiting for someone to SPEAK UP and STEP UP—this starts with you!

#3- During tough times ENCOURAGE those teammates or units that are failing. Urge them to keep fighting!! Support them. Tell them you have their back and know what they are capable of. Offer to join them for extra practice time. Let them know that you believe in them and these tough times will soon pass.

> **BEING ACCOUNTABLE DOESN'T MEAN THAT YOU ARE PERFECT OR PLAY MISTAKE-FREE, IT ONLY MEANS THAT YOU CAN TAKE RESPONSIBILITY AND THAT'S THE FIRST STEP.**

#4- "I may not say much but when I speak, people listen." – If these words come out of your mouth that means you need to SPEAK more often. That means people respect you. That means you have a responsibility.

#5- Invite the team or your position group to your house – extra time together away from the facility helps TREMENDOUSLY. Cook dinner, play video games, watch sports, watch movies, whatever. ANY time that you spend together helps, initiate the effort! Do it on a consistent basis. Set up a weekly tradition.

#6- Leadership is contagious!! Leaders create other leaders. It starts with one—let that be you. Your leadership will cause a ripple effect in your team. If you bring relentless and positive energy to everything that you do they will begin to mirror you.

#7- Eliminate distractions that are holding you back – junk food, video games, academic issues, partying, drama, negative friends. When players see their leaders becoming more serious, they will also begin to sacrifice and make smarter decisions. What you will gain in the future by cutting those distractions will motivate you.

#8- Initiate extra offseason work—bring the energy, set the pace! Have a positive and relentless attitude!! Personal and team improvements happen in the offseason—not during your season! Set the schedule, set the standards, set the positive attitude.

#9- Help your team build trust in each other – no championships are won when a team lacks trust in each other. To be successful, you need teammates that trust each other and a coaching staff who trusts their players. Show your teammates that you trust them. Give your coaches a reason to trust you. Trust begins with simply being where you are supposed to be when you are supposed to be there!

LEADERS NEED TO BE SEEN... AND HEARD! STEP UP + SPEAK UP + SHOW UP!

#10- Come 15 minutes early and stay 15 minutes late – Come to the weightroom or film room on off days and bring your unit or teammates to do quality work, put in the same effort as if your coaches are there. Multiply the extra time by the number of teammates who join you—it adds up quickly!

#11- Show that you CARE – You care about the team and you care about WINNING! Once you decide to quit on your team and just put in minimum effort so will everyone else.

#12- Be in the lockerroom as much as you can, create an environment where team wants to be. Music, attitude, conversation—create a positive environment that people want to hang out in.

#13- Academics – call out younger players who are slipping to get it together – raise expectations for them to be responsible!! They will follow your lead. Make it cool to be on the Honor Roll!

#14- Realize and be sensitive that teammates may have outside issues (family, depression, addiction, injury) going on. Be a listener or supporter. Pull troubled teammates aside. Any distractions off-the-field can keep you away from success; do what you can to help your teammates who are going through off-the-field troubles.

#15- Fights are the biggest reason for suspensions and expulsions (and sometimes losses) – When you see teammates scuffling on or off-campus, break it up or diffuse the situation! If one player fights, usually everyone fights. Be the calming voice in heated situations. You want teammates who are committed and focused enough on winning to walk away.

#16- Go by your coach's offices for 10 minutes a few times a week – spend time with the assistant coaches and coordinators. Get to know your coaches. Ask them what you can be doing to get better.

#17- Hold your teammates to high expectations in every area – if you are successful, they'll listen!

#18- You can be more influential than your coaches, realize that your messages are heard—good and bad.

#19- Cut the nonsense at inappropriate times (meetings, practice, film, lift). If your teammates see that you are serious when you need to be, they will focus too.

#20- Help with recruiting talent once on a college campus—host top recruits, be positive. The coaches are working their butts off to bring in the best players and if you want to win, you should be doing so as well.

#21- Eliminate the negativity in the lockerroom. Establish a NO TOLERANCE attitude for complaining and backstabbing among teammates. Negativity never will win championships. Cut it off immediately! Help feuding teammates to get to the root of their problems and to put them behind them.

#22- Get over losses – be positive and move on – brighter days ahead. Get those around you to believe! Frustration makes quitting easier, get your teammates to PUSH PAST that layer of frustration and focus on doing better the next time.

#23- Get the fans involved, you will need them all season! Appreciate them at school, invite them to games, pump up crowd at key times. Win or lose, thank them for coming!

#24- Talk to your coaches if you or a teammate has a major issue that could hurt team (legal, health, academic, eligibility)—the quicker they hear it, the quicker they can address it – it is what is best for the team.

#25- Praise teammates when they do something great. If you are a leader in front of the media, do it publicly. Don't overdo it but make a point to pat teammates on the back for their improvements. People like recognition and once they begin to get it, they will strive for even more. Motivate the backups and practice players, they don't get much acknowledgement for their hard work.

YOU WILL NEVER EXCUSE YOUR WAY INTO A CHAMPIONSHIP!

10 SACRIFICES YOU CAN MAKE TO BECOME A BETTER PLAYER

#1 – VIDEO GAMES: Put the controller down!!! Play only on the weekend or give them up all together. Use that time during the week for homework or preparing for the ACT or SAT.

#2 – Go out to the field or court 15 minutes early and stay 15 minutes late to get in extra drills every day. Encourage teammates to join you. Extra practice will help you separate yourself if it's taken seriously on a daily basis.

#3 – Stop eating fried foods, processed foods, candy and fast food. Add more fruit and vegetables to your diet.

#4 – Keep your body pure – No drinking, smoking or drugs!

#5 – Make getting enough sleep a priority. Go to bed early and take naps when possible.

DISCIPLINE AND MENTAL TOUGHNESS ARE WANTING TO WIN MORE THAN WANTING TO BE DISTRACTED.

#6 – Wake up an hour early a few times per week to get in extra conditioning. BONUS – Waking up early will help build mental toughness!

#7 – Get position-specific drills in EVERY DAY of the offseason! Ask your coach which drills will help you that you can do on your own. Elite players use the offseason to improve, not just to stay in shape. Select position-specific drills you need improvement on and focus on them every day of the offseason.

#8 – Drink more water! Eliminate sodas and don't overdo it with extra sugar from juice and sport drinks.

#9 – Give up the negative people and influences in your life. Most times, you know exactly WHO and WHAT is holding you back from your dreams and goals. These people and issues are toxic to your future! They are draining you of positive energy which is a NECESSITY on your path to success!

#10 – Get a part-time job (grocery store, mall, restaurant, valet, hospital, construction, moving company) to save up money to attend camps and combines or for travel to visit schools. Do not allow money to be an excuse! A job will also help you build maturity and mental toughness!

14 WAYS TO IMPROVE TIME MANAGEMENT

#1 – Chase greatness and everything else will come – Too many players are too focused on getting all of the media attention and playing the popularity contest that they never develop into great players. They put more focus on those external rewards than becoming great. I've been a part of a BCS National Championship team and worked with Super Bowl Champions and Pro Bowl players, truly great athletes eventually have the world at their feet but they put 99% of their focus on being a beast on the field or court FIRST and know that everything else will come their way. Athletes who chase all of the rewards before they chase championships end up empty-handed!

TOUGHNESS: YOUR SIGNATURE STYLE AS A PLAYER NEEDS TO BE IN YOUR TOUGHNESS, YOUR ABILITY TO WITHSTAND EVERYTHING THROWN YOUR WAY.

#2 – The hardest part about being in a relationship while juggling school and sports is dealing with someone who brings DRAMA to your life! RUN AWAY from dating someone who is constantly picking fights or dragging negative chaos into your life, they only get you worked up, spinning in circles and wasting your energy. They genuinely don't respect the fact that you are trying to accomplish things in your life and will only get worse when success comes your way. A non-drama, healthy relationship won't hold you back from anything, be sure put quality effort into the time you spend with your significant other.

#3 – A majority of problems players run into are self-inflicted. Sure, there are problems you can't help (injuries, family situations) but there are too many other factors that you CAN control. Too many players that I've been around have been brought down by drugs, legal issues, their relationship, laziness or a bad attitude. Be real with yourself and eliminate all of the distractions that you can eliminate. It will be challenging enough to overcome setbacks you can't control, why purposely add extra negativity that you CAN control. If you want success, keep successful people in your circle. If you want drama, spend your time with drama! Don't complain or blame the world when these bad habits come back and take your career away. It will happen!

#4 – Be where you are – If you are with your girlfriend, boyfriend or parents, don't be texting, taking calls or playing video games. Spend quality time with them. If you are working on a paper, don't spend 2 hours arguing with your girlfriend or boyfriend because a paper that can take you one hour to write will take you four or five hours or end up incomplete. Your friends and family will appreciate 100%

of your attention in shorter periods of time than if you are constantly distracted or interrupted.

#5 – Just do what is asked of you the first time. I watch players go in circles all day, trying to get out of extra punishments and trouble they've gotten themselves into, problems they could have avoided by just doing what was asked of them in the first place. Go to class. Go to study hall. Be at practice on time. Be everywhere 5 minutes early and you won't have to worry about detention, punishment workouts or suspensions. If you just do what is asked of you by your teachers and coaches, you will be fine. If you skip class, skip a workout, sleep in class, you will have to face the punishment and that will likely add an extra hour or two to your day.

#6 – TV/Internet– You get sucked in and will go from checking your Facebook 'real quick' to spending 2 hours browsing. Pretend that you are on a diet, you can only have a bite of that cake but you can't eat the whole thing. Don't get sucked into the couch, computer or TV for more than 15 or 20 minutes if you have a big to-do list.

YOU CAN'T LEAD IF NOBODY EVER SEES YOU. YOU NEED TO BE THE FIRST ONE THERE AND THE LAST ONE TO LEAVE!

#7 – Quit talking about how much you have to do and how you'll never possibly get it done and just do it. People yap on and on about how they have too much to do and if they would just shut the door and work on a few things, they will feel a lot less pressure. Put your phone on silent, don't log on the internet, shut your door, go to the library, find a hiding place where you can get your work done and it will eliminate some of the pressure you are feeling.

#8 – Get up an hour early – If you need extra studying or conditioning, get up at 6am and do it. You are much less likely to get distracted by others and as a bonus – it builds mental toughness. If you are can become disciplined enough to get up an extra hour or two earlier you are IMPROVING and building MENTAL TOUGHNESS!

#9 – Are you doing too much? Are you involved in too many sports, clubs, family issues, friend issues? You have to really focus on the two or three things that are really important to you and may have to give up some of the extra distractions that aren't helping you get to where you want to go. For a week, keep track of how much you spend your time on hour-by-hour, you might be surprised.

#10 – Set a study schedule – When I was in college I tried to get to the library Monday-Thursday until 10pm, even if I had no homework due the next day. At times, the library became the hangout spot so I found a different quiet spot on campus to do my work and reading at. There is always work that you can do to get ahead. If you put in the consistent work on those days, you can enjoy the weekend. In college it is near impossible to get any work done in the dorms, go somewhere else and you'll drastically cut the hours you need to finish assignments and prepare, freeing up more time for YOU!

#11 – Prioritize what is important to you. When I was part of a BCS National Championship team – our coach did little outside of developing our players, self-scouting, breaking down opponents, gameplanning, recruiting and creating events or programs that would improve our team. He had his family around the facility often and his wife and kids joined us for dinner after practice sometimes. He rarely got dragged away for fundraising, marketing or other activities unless it meant a big addition to our program. School, sports, family, relationships... Write down your list of a few priorities and focus on the top things that you must have. Everything else, slowly eliminate. If it doesn't help you improve in those areas, drop it.

MOTIVATION IS MORE POWERFUL THAN TALENT ONLY WHEN YOU ARE READY TO COMMIT ON THE HIGHEST LEVEL.

#12 – Put down the video game controller – Save it for the weekend or offseason. Hours, days, weekends are wasted this way!

#13 – Get sleep when you can – Sneak in naps during the day and try to go to bed early. Sleep will help you make fewer mistakes at practice and in games and puts you in a better mood. When you are tired you are cranky and get frustrated and forgetful. It's hard to do everything that is asked and expected of you if you are exhausted. Sneak in naps whenever you can.

#14 – Successful college and pro coaches are some of the most efficient people on the planet. They don't waste a minute. They go from a player meeting to recruit call to film session to scheduling games for next season to planning their travel schedule to checking on their child to a budget meeting with the Athletic Director to a radio phone interview to practice without daydreaming for a minute. It takes that kind of efficiency and focus to become successful on a high level. Are there things you can eliminate from your daily schedule that can cut 10 minutes, 30 minutes or an hour? It all adds up very quickly!

WHEN YOU ACT LIKE YOU DON'T CARE YOU ARE JUST PUTTING UP A WALL BECAUSE YOU DON'T ACTUALLY BELIEVE IN YOURSELF. WINNERS SHOW THAT THEY CARE—WIN OR LOSE!

CHAPTER #10

FINAL WORD: ALWAYS REMAIN IN CONTROL

"People too weak to follow their own dreams typically tend to find a way to discourage yours."

"If you can dream it, you can do it."
– WALT DISNEY

"Your life can't go according to plan if you have no plan."

FINAL WORD: ALWAYS REMAIN IN CONTROL

Your dream is something that you will have to fight for, live for and chase on a daily basis. Don't ever take your foot off the gas, when positive things begin happening for you is when you need to hit the gas even harder. You will have doors slammed in your face and you will likely be underestimated—all of the things that successful people and champions have all faced. You must have a plan, a passion and a purpose and I have hoped to draw that out of you throughout this book.

COACHES CAN'T COACH MATURITY— THAT'S ALL ON YOU! IF YOU WANT TO WIN, YOU HAVE TO GROW UP. It's important to have a dream, chase the goals that everyone tells you that you will never achieve and to keep believing—but it's equally as important to have a solid back-up plan. You never want to leave any offers or opportunities on the table. Remember—no school will ever justify how talented you are, never base your value as a person on who has offered you—you are worth way more than that!

I am here to tell you that no matter what, YOU are the only person who will stop yourself. Not your coaches, your parents, your teammates or your grades. Whenever you feel powerless (which you will at some point, we all do), remember that you always have the power to get an extra work-out in, the power to go for a run, the power to be patient, the power to study harder, the power to work harder, try again and to always have control of your attitude. You need to 'find a way' in everything you do.

FIND a way, MAKE a way, BE RELENTLESS and don't you EVER quit on yourself—no matter how many people try to stand in your way!

Good luck—see you at the finish line!

KEEP CONSTANT, CONSISTENT, POSITIVE AND UNCONDITIONAL FAITH IN YOURSELF!

ABOUT THE AUTHOR

The author has worked with over 70 NCAA Division I coaches over 10 years, competing in eight different sports, as well as professional coaches and athletes, including over than 30 NFL, NBA, MLB 1st Round Draft Picks and several other players who have signed professional contracts. Throughout their career, they have worked alongside players and coaches who have won World Series Championships, Super Bowls, BCS National Championships, NCAA Men's Basketball Titles, NBA Championships, made Final Four Appearances and NFL Pro Bowls, along with individuals who have earned NFL Rookie of the Year honors, Heisman Trophies, National Coach of the Year honors, BCS Championship MVP Awards, NBA All-Stars, Cy Young Winners and both College and NFL Football Hall of Fame Inductees. The author, @1001RecruitTips has put together 'NCAA Recruit Tips' as your blueprint to the college recruiting process, combining these experiences for your guide to develop into the most successful player that you can be!

Made in the USA
Lexington, KY
02 October 2014